HOW TO SET HEALTHY BOUNDARIES

Necessary Self-Care To Help You Feel Freedom, Take Control Of Your Life
And Relationships, And Avoid Being Taken Advantage Of

QATARINA WANDERS PHD

WANDERING WORDS
M E D I A

CONTENTS

Dedicated to all the go-getters and people-pleasers out there who are finally realizing they need to pause and take a deep breath.

WHAT IS LIVING AN UNEDITED LIFE?

Can you imagine what it would be like *not* to feel any boundaries around what you think and dream?

Don't edit yourself.

Allow yourself to go there. To dream BIG.

When you live an unedited life, it means opening your-self up to the world and speaking your truth without fear or judgment. You're not afraid of who might be judging what's on your mind because when you share something with another from the heart—no matter how controversial—all that matters is growing as humans together through unfiltered or "unedited" conversation. Instead of staying silent for anyone else's protection or comfort, speak your truth!

Constantly editing ourselves limits us in our dialogue about what we desire—or difficult subjects and taboo topics such as depression, suicide thoughts, body dysmorphia, open sexuality...we only speak out if like-minded people are around (and then just usually end up complaining and falling into the "victim mindset") which doesn't help anyone feel less alone but rather makes them think there must be something wrong with them since nobody wants anything to do with these conversations.

Living an unedited life is a way of providing open conversation about difficult and taboo subjects without fear or judgment!

Embrace an unfiltered existence while it lasts because there are many who do not have the opportunity to live freely in this manner.

Oh, and hi, I'm Qatarina, I write stuff and talk about taboo subjects. A *lot*. And I will never apologize for that!

The whole "Unedited" brand is something I have been developing over the last few years and revolves around allowing yourself to dream big and allow your fantasies to take shape—all without giving a flying fluff about what anyone else will think about it.

If the nitty-gritty stuff I get into here resonates with you, just know that there is a lot more where this came from. And you don't need coaching to learn all about it. I actually fully intend to share everything I know within

the pages of these books so I can stop coaching alto-
gether. That's my end goal.

But, for now, coaching is giving me powerful new
knowledge and experience every day.

My initial interest in spirituality is what sparked this
journey of empowerment for me. About five years ago,
right after I put out my second book, *Overcoming
Chronic Pain Through Yoga,* I started listening to a
podcast called *The Stream Of David.* It fascinated me
beyond belief. The host of the podcast, David Strickel,
spoke a lot about the law of attraction back then. I was
interested in other law-of-attraction teachings to some
extent, but *The Stream Of David* took it to a whole new
level. David spoke about his Source connection that he
called "the Stream." And the Stream had a lot to say on
pretty much any topic.

In a nutshell, the Stream is the source of all thought
creation. And we are all connected to it in some way.
We all have our own versions of the Stream we can
connect to at any given time—as long as we are aligned
with it and in a positive mental space.

Eventually, David put out an Instagram post looking for
a "spiritually focused book editor," and, because I was
transitioning from full-time health coaching to full-time
book editing at that time (what can I say? I wear a lot of
hats), I applied immediately. He hired me, and the rest

is history. We've been working together ever since, and I worked right alongside him as he created a full-blown online community and what is now called the Tya Practice™. TYA stands for Trust Your Abundance. It holds similar ideas to the law of attraction but allows for a lot more *vibrational flow*. To explain this concept in depth, and to do it any justice, I would have to write another book, and I will (in fact, David and I are co-authoring a book dedicated specifically to the Tya Practice and vibrational flow), or at least dedicate several chapters in my future books, but that's not what this book is about. I only bring all this up to express that the concepts I introduce here are not necessarily mainstream. And some of them may not be well received.

The views I share within these pages come from what the Tya Practice calls a "zoomed out" perspective, and require an extremely open mind. When you're done reading this, if you're still intrigued, there's a lot more where this came from.

The Stream teaches that when you are at a loss in a situation, and you don't know your next step, step back, zoom out, and take fear and judgment out of the equation. If you remove the fear and judgment, what would you do? I apply that to everything in my life now. And especially when it comes to coaching. I coach people from all walks of life. And my clients are all *awesome*.

Anyhoo, if you are interested in learning more about *The Stream Of David* or the Tya Practice, you can check the resources at the back of the book (if you haven't googled it already...like a normal person).

Now let's get real.

INTRODUCTION

THE IMPORTANCE OF TAKING AN HOUR PER
DAY FOR YOURSELF CANNOT BE EMPHASIZED
ENOUGH.

Do you find yourself feeling anxious, frustrated, or even angry when someone asks for a favor? Or do you feel hurt when people don't respect your boundaries? If so, this book is for you. We will look at how to set healthy boundaries with friends, family, colleagues, and even ourselves. We also take a closer look at self-care and what it means for personal growth.

Boundaries are important because they define what is acceptable and unacceptable behavior. Healthy boundaries help you establish a sense of self-respect and emotional safety, which in turn helps build healthy relationships with others.

The time for understanding how to set healthy boundaries has come. You don't have to let anyone take advantage of you ever again.

I know it can seem hard to set boundaries, but if you follow these steps, I promise that they will not only improve your life but also the lives of those you love.

FIRST 3 STEPS TO SETTING HEALTHY BOUNDARIES:

1) Start by listing what's important to you and why.

2) Ask yourself how much time each day would be OK for each person or situation on the list.

3) Make a list of your priorities: things and people who are most important to you, then rank them in order from top priority down to least.

There, that's the gist of it. There is more to it, obviously, but we will get to that. This is only the intro, after all.

This will help build healthy boundaries with friends, family members, coworkers, etc. For example: You want quality time with your significant other but also have an obligation at work every day after lunch, so sometimes that is not possible. Therefore it becomes a "lower" priority than spending quality time with your significant other, which is now "high" priority.

This is because your significant other should be a higher priority than work—your partner is the one you love and want to spend time with, right? If you don't make them a high-enough priority, then it becomes difficult for both parties involved in one of two ways: either they are not happy, or you're unhappy because of the lack of quality time.

If their needs are not important or respected, then they may feel taken for granted or even unloved. They might also start feeling resentful toward you. Setting healthy boundaries shows how much someone means to another person.

The other party in this scenario could become frustrated and angry because their needs are not being met. They might start to feel taken advantage of because they have been giving and giving without getting anything in return, which is why setting boundaries for yourself first is crucial before you set them with others.

I used to work on a hospital floor where there were many different types of people from all walks of life: nurses, doctors, patients, families. I learned to make a list of the people who come into my life and how much time each day is OK for them to take up in order to complete everything that needs to be done.

We had a patient population on my floor where some patients needed more attention than others. But there were nurses who worked 12-hour shifts, meaning that they had a max amount of time to spend with each patient per day.

How could any of this be handled without boundaries?

It couldn't.

I learned a lot about boundary setting at that job. Those nurses were superheroes. And I will share with you what they taught me over the years.

There are many people in my life who want the same thing: quality time, so I need to know what is going on before I can set boundaries for myself and others.

Healthy boundaries help you not only set yourself up for success but also teach other people how to do it as well.

Now let's get into the first three steps in a little more detail...

Step One: Identify what's important and why.

We all want to be looked at as an individual with our own needs, wants, desires, etc., so the first step in setting healthy boundaries is identifying what is important to you and why. What are your goals? Who/what do you need in order to reach those goals? What are your main priorities in life and why? These are all questions to ask yourself to help develop a clearer understanding of what is important to you.

Step Two: Find out how much time per day you must set aside for each person or situation on the list.

Once we know what we want, it's time to set boundaries for ourselves. The next step is to find out how much time per day we need in order to get all of our needs met and be happy with who we are. We can do this by making a list of the people or situations that come into our life on any given day that take up some, if not most, of your time. These people or situations will be ranked on your list depending on how much priority they take up in your life and the time you need for them.

Step Three: Rank each person or situation in order of importance and then prioritize the list.

This is where we start to put it all together. We need to rank our different people, relationships, and situations based on how important they are in your life by assigning a numerical ranking system from one to three (or whatever number you come up with). The number one corresponds with the most important person or situation on your list.

This will ensure that you're spending enough time with each person but also not overdoing it and setting yourself up for failure.

PEOPLE WHO HAVE A SOLID SENSE OF SELF-RESPECT KNOW THEIR OWN NEEDS MATTER.

We go through life trying our best, giving it our all, but there are those times when we need to know it's OK to slow down and rest.

Following these steps will help you create a sense of self-respect, emotional safety, and healthy relationships.

It is important for all individuals involved—you included—to establish a sense of emotional safety through respectful dialogue rather than just an angry outburst, because this helps keep everyone calm and at peace. Once things are sorted out or when someone has overstepped their bounds (again), then there can be consequences from either person involved.

Remember what's important to you and why. It is imperative that you do not let anyone take advantage of your time more than they need to, or else it will lead to an emotional breakdown in the end (I speak from experience). You are worth at least one hour per day for yourself because, without it, you won't be able to function in any other aspect of your life.

You owe this time to yourself and the people around you.

The importance of taking an hour per day for yourself cannot be emphasized enough. It doesn't matter if you're working two jobs, have children at home, or are a full-time student. You owe it to your future self to be present in the moment.

We all have our own needs, but we also need time for ourselves so that we can care for those around us as well. When people know their boundaries, they will respect them more. People who have a solid sense of self-respect know their own needs matter.

Learn how to set healthy boundaries with yourself and others in order to build strong relationships based on mutual respect. Learn more about self-care, what it means for personal growth, and why we need to take care of ourselves first before taking care of others. I promise you that if you follow these first three steps (along with the rest I will introduce throughout the book), not only will your life improve, but the people around you's lives will as well!

Healthy Boundary Tip: Understand your needs as well as the needs of others around you to find a unique balance between personal space and togetherness.

Let's get started!

INVISIBLE BOUNDARIES

WE ALL HAVE BOUNDARIES—IN ALL AREAS OF OUR LIVES—WHETHER WE ARE AWARE OF THEM OR NOT.

YEARS AGO, I GOT INVOLVED WITH SOMEONE I WILL call Danny. Now, something to know about me is that I don't shit-talk my exes (anymore—I wasn't always as careful about that as I am now). But, well, this guy had more issues than anyone I've ever dated. I won't get into all the absurdity that was that relationship (I go into it plenty in my upcoming book, *Trainwreck Relationships And How To Avoid Them*), but I will touch on that relationship's number one issue: boundaries.

Danny and I were both entrepreneurs with heavy ambitions—well, that's a lie actually. He *told* me he was an ambitious entrepreneur when we first met, and I believed him for a few months before I realized that was only true in his imagination. In reality, he was an Uber driver living in a house with a bunch of hippies and doing "spiritual coaching" on the side (although he only had one client—who wasn't even paying him), but we won't get into that.

Long story short, he spent a *lot* of time at my house. His hippie compound was an hour away, so he would drive to my house and spend days at a time with me. I couldn't stay at his place with him because, well, I couldn't leave my daughter alone, plus he didn't have furniture for me to sit on, and their house always stank like body odor and patchouli.

Needless to say, a ton of issues started coming up early on. He didn't live with me, and didn't contribute to my bills, but he was there so much he took liberties like he did. And he was a messy, *messy* boy.

He ate my food without asking (and my daughter's food, causing her to resent him immediately), made huge messes all over the house, and continuously left the lights on and the doors unlocked. Plus he was loud when we were trying to sleep—he was a deep sleeper, so the idea that he couldn't blare music at 2am without pissing us off was foreign to him.

Also, because I worked from home, having him around so much *killed* my productivity. He would walk into my office over and over to ask random questions or make small talk. All. Day. Long. Then complain that I worked too much and didn't give him enough attention.

Whenever I tried to bring these issues up to him, he would throw his hands up in the air and cry out, "Oh my god!" And then usually mutter and grumble about "So many rules!" or "I have to be allowed to live my life!"

I know, I know, I probably sounded like the nagging girlfriend. I tried to be diplomatic and kind about it as best I could, but after a while, and it would just KEEP HAPPENING, I'm sure my tone shortened right along with my fuse.

The interesting part about all this was that, from our very first date, he had exhibited extremely strong boundaries. He had trained to be a therapist in his younger years (but never did anything with that), and had a long history of mental illness. Because of this, he was more than careful to make sure he had consent for everything he did with me on our first date.

He had asked, "Can I sit closer to you?" before he sat next to me and "Can I touch you?" before he held my hand. This is all fine and good in some situations, and for some people, but for me it was a huge turn-off. When I finally got tired of waiting for him to kiss me, I leaned in and made the first move. He reciprocated immediately, and that first kiss was fantastic, but later he told me, "It was inappropriate of you to kiss me without my consent."

... Yeah.

This issue showed up in our sex life early on as well. I had no idea how to make a move on him unless I straight-up asked, "Can we have sex, please?"

NOT sexy at all.

There were also a few times when I tried to kiss him spontaneously, and he jerked away from me and walked off, harrumphing, "I don't want to be touched at this moment!"

So...do you see the boundary issues yet?

He was *all about* boundaries. He enforced them left and right—but only in one area: sexual intimacy/physical touch...toward himself. Invading my living space was a non-issue to him because he didn't have any personal boundaries in that area.

My boundaries were different, and he couldn't understand that.

I did my best to respect *his* boundaries, but I eventually had to admit to myself that it could never work. Having to ask explicit permission to touch my significant other every single time (and frequently being told no) left me feeling inadequate and unloved.

On top of that, having to constantly clean up after someone who told me he didn't believe in compromise —and that it was my choice to clean up after him and therefore made it not his problem—made me feel used and taken advantage of.

Even if we had communicated our boundaries more effectively, that relationship never would have worked. When it came down to it, I couldn't handle his boundaries and he couldn't handle mine.

Lesson learned.

I bring this up to illustrate the opposite ends of the spectrum here. To me, cleaning up after yourself when you track dog shit through your girlfriend's house, and not eating her lunch she had meal-prepped for herself the previous evening, seemed like no-brainers to me. But not to him. He felt confined and controlled.

On the other hand, his seemingly excessive (to me) physical-touch boundaries made me feel completely isolated from him.

Also, I had never consciously set these kinds of boundaries before. I had never even thought about it. My previous partners had never overstepped them, so I had never had to address such things. There were invisible boundaries that came to light in that relationship.

I can't speak for his feelings, because they tended to pendulum back and forth several times a day, but I can certainly speak for my own: his boundaries made me feel disrespected, and his disregard for mine also made me feel disrespected.

Therefore, that relationship was a lost cause. We were absolutely incompatible. And that's OK.

ARE BOUNDARIES IMPORTANT?

This is the million-dollar question. Many happy, thriving individuals get along just fine in life without ever consciously setting boundaries. So maybe they aren't needed, right?

Well...consider this: just because someone has never consciously set a boundary doesn't mean they don't have them. We all have boundaries—in all areas of our lives— whether we are aware of them or not. For instance, do you allow creepy ax-wielding strangers in clown suits into your home? Probably not (just a guess). That's a boundary. Would you let your hairdresser use cow dung instead of hair gel? Nope. That's another boundary.

Okay, so I realize these are extreme—and fairly ridiculous—examples, but my point is that boundaries exist in our lives no matter what. But some people don't ever think about them because they don't need to. And that's all fine and good...for them, but that's not what we are talking about here, is it? No.

You wouldn't be reading this book if you were one of those people. And I wouldn't be writing this book if I were! You probably picked this up because you are having some sort of boundary issues. Perhaps you frequently find yourself feeling taken advantage of. Or maybe you have trouble saying no and find yourself completely overwhelmed with all you said yes to.

Having clear boundaries can help you avoid such situations and can be important in many areas of life: romantic, professional, familial, social, and sexual. They are usually formed fairly naturally by our upbringing, personal beliefs, and feelings, but not always.

Sometimes other dominant personality traits lead the way instead (like wanting everyone to like us), so that's where assessing our boundaries can come into play. So, OK...boundaries...got it. But what exactly *are* they?

WHAT IS A BOUNDARY?

If you are reading this book, you probably already know what boundaries are. But, for the sake of clarity, let's break it down a little.

Merriam Webster defines a boundary as: *something that indicates or fixes a limit or extent.*

Guidelines, rules, and limits one creates to identify for themselves what is reasonable, safe, and permissible behavior in their presence would be considered boundaries.

A boundary is that line where your responsibility to others ends and responsibility to yourself begins. This includes how you respond when someone oversteps this line.

When it comes to our personal lives, a boundary can mean a significant amount of physical and emotional space you allow between yourself and others. This enables you to decide what sorts of interactions and types of communication are acceptable for you.

Boundary-setting is one way to practice necessary self-care and enhance self-respect. When they are well thought out and placed with care, boundaries can help with communication and create space and time for positive interactions.

A BOUNDARY IS THAT LINE WHERE YOUR RESPONSIBILITY TO OTHERS ENDS AND RESPONSIBILITY TO YOURSELF BEGINS.

FOOD FOR THOUGHT

- Can you identify five personal boundaries already in place in your life?
- Are there certain areas in your life lacking boundaries where you need them?
- Try to identify a few boundaries you observe for someone close to you.

Now that we've established what boundaries are, and why they are important, let's get into why some of us need to set them and why others perhaps need to back off a little bit. Is there such a thing as too many boundaries?

THE BOUNDARY WHORE

WHEN YOU SPEND ALL YOUR TIME BUILDING
WALLS, EVENTUALLY THEY CAN BECOME
IMPENETRABLE. WE MAY THINK THAT'S
WHAT WE WANT AT FIRST, BUT IT CAN GET
PRETTY LONELY WITHIN THE BORDERS OF
YOUR OWN FORTRESS.

NOW THAT YOU UNDERSTAND WHAT BOUNDARIES ARE,
why they matter, and how they can help you, ask yourself how they are already at work in your life. Hopefully, you can see the positive effects, but you are probably also starting to see room for improvement, which is great. The next question is, when it comes to boundary setting, how much is too much?

Boundaries help us feel safe, respected, heard, and loved. But what happens when we set too many? Have you ever met someone who died that?

I was running around like a chicken with my head cut off. My dad had just passed away from cancer, and I had taken on more than I could handle. I was already an emotional wreck from losing my father, and I had spent so much time trying to make him proud before he passed that everything just caught up with me as soon as he died.

My seven-year romantic relationship had just ended, I was fighting for custody of my daughter, and I was trying to grow a new business from zero. I don't know what the hell possessed me to try to do all of that at once, but well, that's what happened.

As an overachiever my whole life, I never considered that trying to do everything at once might actually kill me.

I guess I just thought I could handle it. After all, I had up and given up everything in my younger years to literally run away and join the circus, so I thought I was invincible. I'm not kidding. And I will just say, I had never thought about needing boundaries in the circus.

But, after a couple decades of the traveling vagabond life, followed by trying to settle down and be normal, my life had turned into a kerfuffle that I had no idea how to untangle.

I did eventually sort things out, obviously, or I wouldn't be writing this book, but maybe not in the way you may think. I started with setting rigid boundaries for myself to make sure no one could bypass my strict schedule or discipline habits. Yeah, I definitely stayed single for a while because of that.

In hindsight, I went a little overboard. I wanted to be conservative with my time so I could be as productive as possible. I knew self-care was important as well, so any time that wasn't allotted for productivity went to physical activity. Weightlifting and yoga specifically. I figured that was how I needed to maintain my mental health.

I stopped trying to please other people and proceeded to put my blinders on and forge the path ahead of me.

You know what happened?

I had a stroke.

OK, so there *is* such a thing as too many boundaries.

When you spend all your time building walls, eventually they can become impenetrable. We may think that's what we want at first, but it can get pretty lonely within the borders of your own fortress.

So how can we have boundaries with our time, our money, our needs, our human interaction, and even our sexualities? All the while remaining fluid, free, and open to new opportunities? It's totally possible.

In a nutshell, it comes down to going inward and assessing the reason the boundaries are needed in the first place.

There you go. You can put the book down and move on. Just kidding. There's obviously a lot more to it than that, but it does really boil down to the simple concept of personal assessment.

First and foremost, I want to bring up a concept that very few have touched upon, and that is having healthy boundaries with *yourself*. Many thought leaders talk about the importance of self-care, many others talk about the importance of self-discipline, some talk about pushing yourself or going easy on yourself, but what is the happy medium? That's where setting your own personal boundaries can come in.

The idea of healthy boundaries has a lot of judgment attached to it—from both directions. Having too many can make you "unapproachable." Not having enough can make you a "doormat."

Many people tend to lean a little too far in one direction or the other. Finding that balance starts with a few key steps.

FOOD FOR THOUGHT

- Assess why you feel the need to have a boundary in a certain area.
- Determine whether you have created a boundary in the first place, and, if so, where it needs to be versus where it currently is.
- Envision the end result: what will this area of your life look like if you achieve an ideal set of boundaries around it?

Once these actions are taken, move on to assessing another area of your life that could benefit from having some new self-imposed boundaries.

But how do you set such boundaries? Let's get into that next.

HOW TO SET STR

QATARINA WANDERS PHD

In order to ensu... always look ... you; do th... this co... happe...

BOUNDARIES ARE NOT MEANT TO BE A WAY OF CONTROLLING OTHERS, SO MAKE SURE YOU'RE COMFORTABLE WITH THE SITUATION AND WHAT YOU NEED.

IN ORDER TO SET GOOD BOUNDARIES FOR YOURSELF, you need to know who you are, what your values are, and how much of your time and energy is worth spending on projects or other people.

When setting boundaries for yourself, pick one or two values that most resonate with you and create a plan around them. Once everyone knows they have these valuable priorities in their life, it becomes easier for them to set good personal boundaries.

re success when setting said boundaries, it how much time someone has asked of s by asking questions like "Do I really want mmitment?" and "Is there anything else ning that I want/need to do more?"

ter that, stay aware of how you're feeling and if a person is respecting your boundaries. There's no point in saying anything if they don't respect it, so take a step back or try setting limits again.

Setting personal boundaries takes time, patience, and consistency, but with the right approach, anyone can do it.

Take a moment to think about how you might handle the following situations:

- Tired from work? Maybe that means less TV for today. (Boundary with yourself.)
- Seems like your daughter has been using your credit card without permission. What should you do? (Boundary with children.)
- Sharing custody: What are some good ways to set healthy parental boundaries when working on parenting agreements? (Boundaries with friends and those we have friction with.)
- Your partner wants to watch TV in bed, but that keeps you awake. Do you say something? (Relationship boundary.)

- A coworker keeps leaving for the day without completing everything they are supposed to. Do you pick up the slack? (Boundaries at work.)

Mull these over. There is no right or wrong answer, but it is good to think about how these scenarios would play out for you (if they haven't already) and where you might need to make adjustments.

Finally, here are some guidelines to help you set boundaries for yourself:

- Treat your own needs as important.
- Be conscious of the time and energy it takes to meet those needs.
- Recognize that what is most important to you should not be an obligation or burden on others. Your decisions, values, and feelings need to matter too.
- Keep in mind that intimacy requires space; there's a difference between being close with someone and giving them all your attention. You can create healthy boundaries by understanding when enough closeness has been reached, without always needing more. It's OK if someone else wants less contact than you do, but make sure there's room for both people in this relationship. And know how much contact is enough for both of you.

This is a problem that can't be solved with one solution to work for everyone. Do your best to understand what you are going through and how it may affect the way you handle situations at home, in school, or on the job. For example: How much of an inconvenience would this situation cause? What does this person bring into your life to be worth the trouble? If you are feeling overwhelmed, it's OK to say something, but there is no cookie-cutter answer.

Boundaries are not meant to be a way of controlling others, so make sure you're comfortable with the situation and what you need.

However, if you set too many boundaries, people might think that they don't matter to you. Know your needs and what is most valuable for yourself so that others can learn from it. If someone isn't respecting your space then it's time to speak up about how this makes you feel or if there are any other ways they can be of help to you. Just do it kindly.

FOOD FOR THOUGHT

- Address issues with kindness and patience; if you can't, then wait until you can.
- Treat yourself with care—no one will respect your boundaries if you don't respect your own.

- Be conscious of your time and energy investments.
- Recognize that what is most important to you should not be an obligation or burden on others.
- Keep in mind that intimacy requires space; there's a difference between being close with someone and giving them all your attention.

In the next chapter, we will discuss boundary violations and how to deal with them.

BOUNDARY VIOLATIONS

BOUNDARIES ARE PERSONAL. WHAT MIGHT BE GOOD FOR ONE PERSON MAY NOT BE RIGHT FOR THE NEXT.

A BOUNDARY VIOLATION OCCURS WHEN SOMEONE HAS done something that you find unacceptable, disrespectful, or hurtful. It could be a friend who doesn't return your phone calls when they said they would and then ignores all of your messages without apologizing even though (from your perspective) they were wrong to do so.

Solutions depend on the situation, but a few ideas are listed below:

- Remind them how important it is to follow through on their promises—no matter what.
- Share your feelings when you feel you have been mistreated. You might say something like "I felt ignored when you didn't call me back after you said you would because..."
- If they continue to take advantage of your boundaries, remove yourself from the situation. For example, if they come over unannounced or without notice, telling them that this will not be tolerated, and if it continues, that's it for the friendship.

A healthy boundary can be an agreement that a friend or loved one will not interrupt you when you're resting. It can also be telling someone that you will not be giving them any more favors because they take advantage of your time. It can be uncomfortable or awkward sometimes, but as people learn this is an important part of who you are, they will alter their behavior accordingly—or exit your life.

Yes, it can be uncomfortable when someone violates these agreements and disregards your wishes. What's the solution? Set new boundaries for yourself (or reinforce old ones) by telling this person what type of behavior is unacceptable to you. If they continue to violate those boundaries, let them know in no uncertain terms that their actions are hurting you: "I refuse to allow anyone else into my space." And remember—you are worth it!

You should never have to feel like there's "no point in saying anything" because sometimes people really don't get it.

Healthy Boundary Tip: Understanding your needs as well as those around you to find balance between personal space and togetherness starts today! Let's start exploring some common boundary violations...

WHAT ARE SOME COMMON BOUNDARY VIOLATIONS?

- When a friend asks for help, but they get angry when you say no.
- Someone interrupts you while resting and doesn't respect your time.
- Someone violating time limits by turning up unannounced at a party, or coming in without knocking on someone's door (or any other kind of entrance that has been set as off limits).
- Having someone go through your personal belongings without permission or asking for consent to enter (ex: closets, drawers, journals).

- Someone pushing you past the boundaries of what is agreed upon between both parties when it comes to physical boundaries such as touching, hugging, etc.
- Constant requests for favors—especially when they ask repeatedly and then get angry if you don't comply with the request.

People have different limits when it comes to their personal space and what they allow others around them to do or not.

Learn how to address these violations by making it clear that your needs matter and you will not tolerate being taken advantage of.

WHAT ARE SOME HEALTHY BOUNDARIES TO SET?

- If someone is asking too much of you or not respecting your time... You might want to tell this person that from now on, only X then Y times per week would work best and make sure that everyone involved understands what these new limits mean for all parties. This ensures balance between personal space and togetherness.
- Making time for yourself and your needs every day (e.g., by keeping a planner or setting reminders on your phone).

- Being able to say "no" without feeling guilty or obligated (e.g., if you don't want to do something, it doesn't matter the reason).
- If you have a tendency to overeat, not allowing yourself to eat in front of the TV.

Boundaries are personal. What might be good for one person may not be right for the next. It's important to think about what feels safe and comfortable, then do your best to make that happen.

There are all sorts of healthy boundaries to be aware of in your life. Some people have trouble setting any at all, while others find it easy because they know exactly which ones suit them best. But if you're not sure, then you can figure it out by taking a look around and seeing where you or others get hurt or offended.

For example, food is something that's easy to take advantage of, so make sure your boundaries are clear when it comes to what and how much food you're eating. This includes time as well—don't let others put an unhealthy pressure on you to change your schedule habits. And finally, boundaries with feelings and emotions—like when others leave you feeling guilty or if they pressure you into something that makes you uncomfortable.

Healthy Boundary Tip: Get out of the mindset that's keeping you stuck. You deserve to be treated with respect, so let people know what is or isn't OK... But don't try to control other people by setting *too many* boundaries.

One's limits are a little different for everyone, but it's usually when they act out that we know something is wrong. Listen to what someone has been experiencing and how they have been behaving as an indicator of where their limit may exist.

The effects should never be underestimated. Boundaries keep you on your path, as well as help establish a sense of self-respect and respect among others.

The best thing you can do is take a deep breath, create healthy boundaries, and stick with them. Remember that this person may have their own set of needs and reasons for acting the way they are. But if your boundaries continue to be violated or ignored after doing everything in your power to stop it from happening, then you should know what else to expect—so a discussion in needed.

FOOD FOR THOUGHT

- How do you respond when a friend asks for a favor? Don't feel pressured into agreeing because feeling obligated to do things for people you don't want to can be a form of control.
- What are you willing, or not at all willing, to tolerate in your relationships with others?
- How have you handled boundary violations in the past?
- Can you think of instances where you have violated another's boundary?

Are there ways to make sure these boundaries occur naturally instead? Let's explore more about these next...

THE BOUNDARYLESS RELATIONSHIP

INDIVIDUALS WITH A HEALTHY LEVEL OF SELF-WORTH CREATE, LIVE BY, AND ASSERT BOUNDARIES NATURALLY, AS WELL AS RESPECT THOSE OF OTHERS.

THE IDEA OF CREATING A BOUNDARY IS ABOUT detuning the lack of worthiness, or the neediness, surrounding that particular area. Understand that in your higher appreciation of yourself, the boundaries will be natural. In fact, you won't feel like you are imposing them at all.

If that sounds far-fetched, don't worry. This is a major concept that takes a lot of time to grasp. In a utopian paradise, no one needs boundaries because everything just "flows." But, realistically, we probably need to put in some work before we can get to that point.

When boundaries are put into place naturally, it comes from being in a place of security without such need of appreciation of another person.

Remember how I mentioned those people who have never even considered consciously setting boundaries? Those are the people who have figured this step out. It all comes down to self-worth. Individuals with a healthy level of self-worth create, live by, and assert boundaries naturally, as well as respect those of others.

Taking this a little further, when we look deep at our own situations, are we showing others the same level of appreciation we want them to show us? Observing boundaries in another is just as important when it comes to creating one within our own lives. Yes, boundaries are important for maintaining our own self-care and maybe even our sanity, but clearing the desperate need for boundaries is the first area to address when it comes to setting them naturally.

When you can get rid of the attachment to pleasing people, or desperately avoiding upsetting others, it's easy to relax into your own groove. If you can accept that the feelings and actions of others have nothing to do with you, then boundaries do indeed begin to set themselves naturally.

Whenever there is an issue with a boundary, there is always an underlying issue of why you are allowing the issue—the *lack* of the boundary. This gets into the *need* of the situation or relationship. If you are confident in your solo flight, confident in yourself, without needing another's approval, appreciation, or encouragement, the energy of needing the other dissipates. This in turn dissipates the energy that makes you feel you need to set boundaries in the first place. Because by this point, the boundaries just become a natural aspect of the relationship or situation. This also goes for wishing to avoid disapproval or friction. **If you take fear and judgment out of the equation, what are you left with?** How would you operate if fear and judgment weren't a factor?

When you strip a situation down to its roots like this, you can find the need for boundaries in the bare bones. And then, eventually, the boundaries are just naturally there.

When you stop worrying about what others will think or say, you are taking care of *you* first. And that's more than OK; in fact, it's empowering.

Although a boundaryless relationship does not exist, if you continue to de-tune fear and judgment, the need for boundary-setting in the first place will no longer exist either.

To express your needs to others or just say no, you can say it in a clear and assertive way.

If you're confused about what to do with boundaries, you can take some time for yourself and meditate on the boundary and how it's going to work for you. If you're still not sure of the boundary, then take some more time for self-reflection and think about how best to set and address it.

The expression of needs is about releasing fear and judgment, not the other way around.

This framework is a great place to start and will be more helpful than you may have realized.

We just need some work before we can get there, but it's never too late.

The next step is not only understanding our own needs on how we communicate these boundaries with others, but to understand the needs of others as well. If we're going to set boundaries in a way that is respectful and helpful, both parties need clear understanding on what those are.

We can do this by asking ourselves: "What would I like if it was me?"

This framework also applies when you feel like someone has overstepped a boundary with you. Try to understand the other person's needs.

Understanding your own boundaries is crucial before understanding the other person's needs and what would be best for them as well.

This framework will give you a lot of tools to use in both situations, while also learning how to communicate these needs more effectively without fear or judgment being an issue. This way it becomes a natural part of the relationship.

THE ROLE FEAR PLAYS

When you are operating in a place of fear, fear is the thing holding you back from being completely honest on any topic including your desire to have your space—your desire to be more independent.

If you are not confident in your solo flight, if there is any underlying lack of confidence that leads to the need for boundaries (i.e., fear and judgment), then this will be present when setting or discussing boundaries with others as well.

There's always an underlying issue at play whenever a boundary needs resetting.

Fear is a natural response to any unknown situation, but fear should not be something that holds you back from trying new things or opening up to others. Fear can actually help drive us forward when we take it on as an opportunity rather than a barrier.

If there are other emotions at play like resentment, anger, or other "negative" emotions that are being directed at others, then this is the time to make a change before those feelings continue.

THE ROLE JUDGMENT PLAYS

Judgment is not about whether you're more "right" than anyone else. It's just about taking care of yourself first by judging what you need.

Your needs are important and should be heard, not silenced—whether you're giving them or taking them on yourself.

This framework is here for a couple of reasons: to show that judgment can come from both directions (giving and receiving) as well as showing the importance in setting boundaries when it comes to emotions that are being directed at others.

DEALING WITH FEAR

Fear can actually help drive us forward when we take it on as an opportunity. If there are other emotions at play then this is the time to make a change before those feelings continue.

The idea that you must achieve certain things, and that you must put forth a specific image to the world, or your partner, or your friends, or your coworkers...detuning all of that will help you detune your judgment of yourself.

The exploration of all these things is interconnected. When you take the time to explore why it's so important for you to achieve certain things, and that you must put forth a specific image to others, you will find the roots in fear and judgment here as well.

It's not your fault that, at one point in time, being perfect or having people like who they are with was a priority.... The problem is thinking of this as the truth over and over again without ever taking time to question its validity. When you take on this belief system, it becomes true.

Remember this is all an imperfect journey. And we have to remember to feel worthy even when everything isn't exactly as the world tries to convince us it should be.

If you're not happy with your life, explore what makes you unhappy and start taking steps toward making those things different in your daily practice. Start by accepting that change is a constant and that nothing is permanent.

THE POINT IS NOT PERFECTION

This whole concept of "taking care" isn't about perfection. It's not about trying to be perfect in another's eyes. And it's not about getting everything right all the time and never making mistakes.

The point is that we are constantly evolving and growing, which means there will always be something for you to take care of or improve on. There will always be more work to do in order to express yourself as fully and authentically as possible.

When you craft your solutions, you create your own point of expansion.

Instead of focusing on the problem, try looking at it from the point of view of the solution.

We're all constantly evolving. And that's the point of this framework—to explore how we can take our judgmental behavior and become less judgmental with ourselves and others by taking care of what needs to be heard rather than silenced.

You are not your job. You're not who you were in high school, where you grew up, how much money is in your bank account, or what car you drive. It's all just stuff and doesn't define the true meaning of life, which can only be found within yourself.

What does this look like for us? What does it mean to become the person we want to be?

It's about taking risks, exploring new horizons, and remembering that anything is possible when you take a leap of faith.

FOOD FOR THOUGHT

- Boundaries are about detuning the lack of worthiness or neediness surrounding a particular area.
- Boundaries come from being in a place of security without such need for appreciation.
- Individuals with healthy self-esteem create boundaries naturally and respect those of others when they have boundary issues because they know there is an underlying issue that needs to be addressed.
- Boundaries are about removing the need to please or avoid upsetting someone else, and when we strip a situation down to its roots, boundaries naturally exist because this is what people want all along.
- Boundaries should not be used as a crutch, but just an expression of who you are and your values. These boundaries will then naturally come into place in the context of relationships because they're what people really want all along.

- Individuals with boundary issues will benefit from addressing the underlying issue that caused the need for boundaries in the first place.

UNDERSTAND THAT IN YOUR HIGHER APPRECIATION OF YOURSELF, THE BOUNDARIES WILL BE NATURAL. IN FACT, YOU WON'T FEEL LIKE YOU ARE IMPOSING THEM AT ALL.

Consider this chapter the most important one in this book. If you were to read only one chapter, this would be the one to apply to your life that would give you the greatest results.

Perhaps even read it again now.

PERSONAL BOUNDARIES

HAVING BOUNDARIES WITH YOURSELF MEANS NOT BEING AFRAID TO DO THINGS THAT ARE DIFFERENT OR OUTSIDE OF THE NORM IN ORDER FOR YOU TO BE TRUE TO WHO YOU REALLY ARE.

SOMETIMES PEOPLE DON'T DO WHAT THEY WANT because they're afraid that others might judge them negatively or reject them in some way. This type of attitude doesn't allow anyone to be themselves or live their best life and get the things they truly desire.

So, therefore, the consequences of not having healthy boundaries with yourself are that you might be afraid to do what you want because others may judge or reject you.

Get this mindset out of your head and stop letting others run your life. NOW. It doesn't matter if someone judges or rejects you because they're not the ones who have to live with yourself on a day-to-day basis like you do. You deserve happiness, so don't allow anyone else to take that away from you.

Life is all about risk. It's important to take chances and live life without fear of what other people might think —that way you're living in your highest vibe. Having boundaries with yourself means not being afraid to do things that are different or outside of the norm in order for you to be true to who you really are.

It may feel like an uphill battle at times, but once you start setting them, and stick with it, your life will change dramatically. They'll help you have healthy relationships, make sure your needs are met, and prevent people from walking all over you.

Setting boundaries is a major part of self-care because it helps us to respect ourselves so that we're not mistreated by others or made to feel victimized in any way.

WHY SHOULD YOU HAVE BOUNDARIES WITH YOURSELF?

Having boundaries with yourself means that you're not afraid to do things outside of the norm for fear of what others might think. Zoom out your perspective, take risks, and live your life without being afraid.

Living a life based on what other people feel or want is never going to work out in the long run. Live for yourself and not what others want you to be. Trust me. It's the way to go. But yeah, I realize it sounds easy on paper—maybe not so much in day-to-day life.

It's never going to work out in the long term if your life is based on how other people want you to be, because then it becomes about them instead of being true to who you really are.

I always said to myself that I would never live my life for what other people wanted me to be.

Did I always follow through with that? Well, no, not exactly. But that's OK. I just had to do a lot of course-correction sometimes.

Sometimes it seemed like everyone around me was getting their way, and I felt more alone than ever before.

I became jealous of those who had that kind of fortune because they were able to control others through manipulation or by using guilt as a weapon. It was like they had power over me because I didn't know how to say no.

I eventually realized that was *my* problem—I felt weak and powerless, but it took some time for me to develop the courage inside myself. I had to yank myself out of that victim mindset. Then one day, when someone said something negative about who I am as a person, I finally found my voice again.

The reason it seemed like everyone around me got their way was because I couldn't speak up for myself. I believed them. I was ashamed of what they accused me of and thought I needed to change it.

It took me some time to fully come into my voice again and speak up for myself, but when that certain someone said something about me, it was different than before.

I found the courage inside of me on that day because I stopped letting all the pointless crap bother me. They could believe whatever they wanted—and that was *their* problem, not mine.

WHAT DOES IT MEAN TO HAVE "HEALTHY" VERSUS "UNHEALTHY" BOUNDARIES?

Having healthy boundaries with oneself means not allowing others to overstep their bounds. Be true to who you really are and don't let anyone control, manipulate, guilt-trip, or judge you for it.

It can be hard living without fear of what other people might think because, as I mentioned, the constant need for approval and fear of rejection can be overwhelming.

A person with healthy boundaries:

- values their own opinions, does not bargain or compromise values for others;
- discusses the reasons for boundaries and how to create them;
- lays out their personal information in a way that is appropriate and safe;
- has learned their wants and needs, and knows how to communicate these effectively;
- knows to hold firm when others push or give in.

Healthy boundaries are based on the opinions of *oneself.*

A person with *unhealthy* boundaries:

- might tease or act out against a person who is withdrawn;
- blurts out personal information;
- finds it difficult to say no when other people make requests;
- is overly invested in other people's problems;

- accepts abuse and breaks personal rules for a person in order to please them.

FOOD FOR THOUGHT

- Be content about who you are in the world and what you want.
- Stop letting others control your life.
- Allow yourself to be a better person by following your instincts.
- Follow your heart and live unapologetically.
- You don't have to be afraid of judgment or rejection.

In summary, a person with healthy boundaries values their own opinions, does not bargain or compromise values for others, and has learned the wants and needs of themselves. A person with unhealthy boundaries might word-vomit personal information without being asked to do so, and they might break personal rules in order to please another person.

In the next chapter, we'll discuss what it takes to develop strong boundaries in a world that seems bent on compromising them.

BOUNDARY AUDIT

BOUNDARIES ARE ALWAYS OPEN TO DISCUS-
SION IF PROBLEMS ARISE AT ANY TIME; IT'S
NOT ABOUT BLACK OR WHITE BUT ABOUT
FINDING THE RIGHT BALANCE.

IT IS FROM TIME TO TIME NECESSARY TO RE-EXAMINE boundaries and also make some changes. The last step after deciding on a boundary, setting up the boundary, and communicating the boundary, is following through. This can include noticing if it's been kept or broken at all times as well as responding when it gets broken (i.e.: an appropriate consequence, talking through a conflict).

WHAT ARE SOME WAYS THAT PEOPLE HANDLE BOUNDARIES ON THEIR OWN?

It can be beneficial for someone who often feels like they're being taken advantage of by others and doesn't feel fulfilled in a relationship to create specific limits with regards to what they're willing to do.

It can also be helpful for partners who have opposing wants and needs in a relationship to take turns compromising, because that way everyone gets what they want individually while still being together as an actual couple.

Boundaries are always open to discussion if problems arise at any time; it's not about black or white but about finding the right balance.

It's important to know what you're comfortable with and not be afraid to say it, even if that means someone might get mad or upset in the process.

Re-examining boundaries is an ongoing process and one needs support from people closest to them for this work. Professionals can also be a useful part of this process as well (i.e.: counselor, therapist) to help people determine the real cause and effect of their boundaries.

Boundaries are important in any relationship, whether it be personal or professional. Healthy boundaries should always be respected—everyone deserves to have their own opinions heard without being pressured from others.

After a thorough re-examination, it's time for an audit. And this has nothing to do with taxes.

THE BOUNDARY AUDIT

"Whoa!" you might say. "What is this? A magical boundary audit? What does that even mean?"

If you've never given any thought to the question of boundaries, then a boundary audit might be just what you need. This will help you figure out whether or not there are areas in your life where it feels like someone has crossed your mental and emotional barriers without permission. If so, then that person was violating an important part of who we are as humans: our personal space.

A boundary audit is when individuals take inventory on how they feel about their own well-being and set clear limits for themselves (or don't). It could look something like this:

I am taking back my power by asking people if I can touch them before doing so. I do not agree with being touched unless physically consented by both parties.

I will not allow someone to take advantage of me and my feelings in any way, shape, or form.

If I am unable to speak up for myself, then _____ (fill in the blank with a loved one) is going to be there for me as an advocate/support system.

There are many ways people can cross our boundary lines without permission. It's important that we understand how this makes us feel so it can be fixed right away by apologizing for crossing the trust between each other when necessary.

If someone breaks a boundary, then it can make us feel very uncomfortable. It feels like we have to live in this person's world when they don't want us there at all. We will feel embarrassed and scared that the other party thinks less of us because they didn't respect our feelings or space. And if what was done was something sexual, then we will feel victimized and unsafe.

If someone crosses a boundary with us without permission, and they are *not* sorry for it, then there's no point in talking about how what happened makes us feel or if we want to make amends. In this case, the best thing to do is protect ourselves by removing ourselves from the situation and focus on taking care of ourselves.

In many cases, if someone crosses a boundary with us without permission and they *are* sorry for it, then there is still no point in talking about how what happened makes us feel or if we want to make amends (after it has already been addressed at least once) because this person already knows that what they did was wrong.

Remember: the point of this conversation is not to make the other person feel bad about what they did, but rather it's a way for us to get healthy and move on.

FOOD FOR THOUGHT

- Healthy boundaries are based on the opinions of oneself.
- Boundaries should be respected and not crossed by others because they help people feel better about themselves as well as those around them.
- Healthy boundaries can lead to a healthier life for both you and your loved ones, so maintain them at all times.

Yes, boundaries are of the utmost importance, now, in the next chapter, we will get into how to apply these boundaries.

GET CLEAR

A BOUNDARY AUDIT CAN GO A LONG WAY IN CLARIFYING WHERE YOUR LIMITS ARE AND HOW TO ENFORCE THEM MORE EFFECTIVELY. BECOME AWARE OF THE PEOPLE, PLACES, OR THINGS THAT CAUSE YOU STRESS AND ANXIETY.

DO YOU KNOW WHERE THE BOUNDARIES OF YOUR property are? Because I didn't either until my neighbor came over and started building a wall.

I'm not joking. This actually happened.

You should have seen the look on my face when I came home from work one day to find this person laying down cement blocks in my yard and telling me that they owned half of it. Luckily, I had proof of where the boundaries were because we had them surveyed years prior, so there was no confusion over what part belonged to me.

But still...holy crap. That was a surprise.

But it's not just our homes that have boundaries. It is also everything else we own and love: furniture, clothes, electronics—you name it!

One of the most challenging parts about setting limits on what we will allow others to do with things we consider ours is when people try to justify their actions by saying, "I paid for it."

The problem with this is that we are not always talking about things like your car, TV, or sofa—all of which you can get a claim on. We're talking about the boundaries of our space and feelings and how they relate to other people's as well.

It might be hard to understand, but some people feel entitled enough to take over our space without permission.

I'm sure you've been in a situation where you had to call someone out on this because otherwise, your private place would have turned into a public space.

If they come into your home and use the toilet or brush their teeth in your sink without permission, this is called a boundary violation because it's not only crossing over our physical property but also violating personal boundaries of privacy—which are just as important to us (if not more) than any other type of boundary we have.

WHEN BOUNDARIES ARE CROSSED

Once again, if things go unspoken, there might be a chance for someone else to take advantage of us in the future. This is why it's important that we understand how this makes us feel so it can be fixed right away by apologizing for crossing the trust between each other when necessary.

A boundary audit can go a long way in clarifying where your limits are and how to enforce them more effectively. Become aware of the people, places, or things that cause you stress and anxiety. If you notice yourself feeling angry, resentful, or guilty at all, this could be a sign there's something going on outside of your control.

THE WORK-LIFE JUGGLE

Your work-life balance will improve once you set some limits. For example, finding work-life balance in a culture that doesn't value the importance of family time. Set limits on your screen time and when you'll respond to email so as not to feel pressured during important moments with loved ones, or let people know ahead of future business trips where they can find you, but when planning personal vacations, you may want to handle this differently.

The key is to know where those boundaries are. If it's not clear what your limitations should be then a good place to start would be figuring out how much time and focus each aspect of your life needs so that there isn't any overlap or neglecting one thing for another.

This will get better when you establish personal guidelines on what works best for yourself in terms of setting priorities between different aspects like family vs. career etc. However, this can vary depending on who we're talking about—people with fewer responsibilities may need less strict rules while others might have difficulty juggling multiple things at once without them overlapping, which could lead to feelings such as resentment developing if there's too much time spent on one aspect and not enough of another.

But let's be clear about something: a work-life balance is a terrible phrase. It implies that work and life are two separate things, which they aren't.

Honestly, every time I read the phrase "work-life balance," my brain imagines a person riding an office chair down a hill. But I digress...

The key is to know where those boundaries are, but sometimes it's difficult when you're a perfectionist or over-achiever, since these types of people spend most their waking hours working, which in turn can lead them to neglect other parts of life.

If we think back to the point made earlier on how important boundaries are for our loved ones—it's just as true for ourselves. If someone else crosses your boundary lines then let them know firmly and clearly what behavior is unacceptable. It doesn't matter who did what so long as the same rules apply in the future.

It's not always easy to establish these guidelines because you may have difficulty figuring out where your limits are and how they should be enforced, but it's worth it when you can find what works best with little time spent struggling over whether those rules should be more strict or less so.

It's really hard to live a healthy life when you're constantly working. Working while trying to maintain a balance between your personal and professional lives can be difficult at times, but setting some clear boundaries will help with this issue immensely. When it becomes too much of an effort completing daily tasks on time just because you have so many other jobs pulling from your plate—take the opportunity now: give up one or two things that aren't essential, free up more hours in the day (or night) by switching out certain habits like watching TV before bedtime, making healthier meal selections during lunch breaks instead of eating fast food every day...whatever works for each individual person.

Setting guidelines gives us a sense of balance within our lives. Not only does this help with work-life but also other relationships we have such as friends/family members etc., since they'll be aware of how much time can be invested into each relationship—without neglecting an aspect like career because there are no clear limits established beforehand based on personal needs/circumstances.

I've found that the best way to increase your "balance" is through setting limits about how much time you'll set aside for certain tasks. For example, I allot 40 minutes a day for social media.

And finally, it's also important to understand *why* we set boundaries. Boundaries are a way of protecting ourselves from situations where people who want something more than we're willing or able to give them in that moment. It might not feel like it now, but they will help you in the future. If you find yourself feeling angry and resentful at all times, this could be your body's way of telling you there's an issue outside of your control that needs addressing, so just remember: I'm not saying you need to be a self-centered jerk. I am, however, recommending that you get rid of some people in your life if the relationship is draining rather than serving you.

COMMUNICATE CLEARLY

Establish clear boundaries and enforce them consistently. You may need to be more explicit about rules that are difficult to communicate otherwise, such as when you'll be available for work conversations or when you'll take on a project while on vacation. If someone disregards the boundary, one of two things needs to happen: either give a gentle reminder or make a harsh consequence for breaking the rule. Sure, you don't want to be self-centered, but it's also not okay when someone else is constantly violating your boundaries without any repercussions.

The best way of doing this is by understanding your needs, and then figuring out the best way of communicating them to your family/friends/co-workers, etc.

FOOD FOR THOUGHT

- We should establish clear boundaries and enforce them consistently.
- If someone disregards the boundary, either give a gentle reminder or make a harsh consequence for breaking the rule.

- It's easy to be inspired by others' limits, but don't copy them. They're an excellent way for you to think outside the box and come up with truly innovative ideas of your own.
- It's important to set limits, but not so much that you're literally setting a limit on what someone can say, think, or do.
- The best way of doing this is by understanding your needs, and then figuring out the best way of communicating them to your family/friends/co-workers, etc.

In summary, be honest with yourself about what you need in order to maintain balance in your life. By setting boundaries and limits for how much time you'll set aside for certain tasks, you'll find that you're able to accomplish more while still having a healthy work-life balance (if there actually were such a thing).

HOW TO SAY NO

"DARING TO SET BOUNDARIES IS ABOUT
HAVING THE COURAGE TO LOVE OURSELVES,
EVEN WHEN WE RISK DISAPPOINTING
OTHERS. WE CAN'T BASE OUR OWN WORTHI-
NESS ON OTHERS' APPROVAL."

— BRENÉ BROWN

IF YOU'RE ANYTHING LIKE ME, THEN SAYING "NO" HAS always been difficult.

I'm an introvert who despises conflict, and I don't want to disappoint anyone. But there are a few reasons why it's important to say no (at least sometimes). In this chapter, we'll explore these reasons and learn how to start saying no in more healthy ways.

Saying no can be difficult because:

- we are afraid of conflict or hurting the other person's feelings;
- it may not be something that has happened before;
- we don't want to disappoint others, or feel like a letdown, but this is relevant for everything that you do in life. There will always be other opportunities down the line if we say no to this opportunity.

But there are a few reasons why saying no can benefit us:

- Saying no sets boundaries and can help to prevent overcommitment.
- Saying no is about us as well—we need time for ourselves.
- Saying yes all the time often leads to burnout/stress.
- Saying no can free up space for us to do the things we want.
- It's a form of self-preservation, as it helps you maintain your own mental and physical health.

There are many different ways in which you can say no —all depending on the circumstances and your personality.

- Saying no can involve completely declining something, saying you'll do it later, or doing a different task instead (maybe one that is more enjoyable).
- It may also be as simple as asking for an extension on deadlines—this doesn't mean you have to say no outright, but sometimes it might be a good idea to ask for more time.
- Saying no can also involve asking people what they think, and then telling them that you'll do it if everyone agrees—this is an easy way of saying no without the conflict.
- It might also mean giving other suggestions or finding alternatives by brainstorming with someone else.
- It can mean making a different choice, or deciding to do something else.
- Saying no might involve being assertive and telling the person in question how you feel about their request or what they are asking of you—this is an important step because it shows that we care enough not just say yes simply for the sake of saying yes.

PREPARE FOR PUSHBACK

Increasing the number of times you refuse can help build up your "no" muscle. Say no to a server, for example, and he or she won't feel upset. Say no when a vendor tries to sell you something or say no out loud at home.

Establishing boundaries is often met with negativity, but this is a sign that you are succeeding in establishing your boundaries. When faced with a difficult situation, remember to put up your guard and react rationally versus emotionally.

For example, employees are always happier and more productive when they set personal limits. That respect comes from knowing you're respecting yourself, too.

Bestselling author and researcher Brené Brown says, "Daring to set boundaries is about having the courage to love ourselves, even when we risk disappointing others. We can't base our own worthiness on others' approval."

TAKE TIME TO RESPOND

One way to retrospectively determine whether you are too overworked is practicing the art of pausing. For example, if your boss offers you a last-minute business trip and asks for a response immediately, before agreeing to take it, take a quick breath and do some introspection to see how this decision will affect the future. If it seems like it will be a difficult yes, then this is your opportunity to say no.

When you find yourself saying no, don't beat yourself up for doing so. It's a sign that you care about your own needs, and when people around you are aware of this, they're more likely to respect the boundaries as well—or come up with an alternative that still works for everyone.

When faced with difficult situations at work or in life, remember the importance of boundaries and reacting rationally instead.

FOOD FOR THOUGHT

- Saying no can be difficult, but it's an important thing to practice and get better at. Find different ways in which you can say no without feeling guilty about doing so—whether that means declining something outright or suggesting other alternatives.
- When you find yourself saying no, don't beat yourself up for doing so. It's a sign that you care about your own needs.

- Prepare For Pushback: When someone says no to you, they're giving you an opportunity to think about how your request affects them.
- Practicing the Art of Pausing: If someone is asking for something unreasonable or demanding without consideration of your boundaries and needs, that's a good time to say no.

Saying no can be difficult, but it's a form of self-preservation, as it helps you maintain your own mental and physical health.

Now that we have covered establishing the boundaries themselves, I want to get into how boundaries come up in different life situations...

ROMANTIC RELATIONSHIPS

BOUNDARIES OFFER A SENSE OF SECURITY
FOR BOTH YOU AND YOUR PARTNER. THEY
CAN GIVE EACH OF YOU THE FREEDOM TO BE
YOURSELVES WITHOUT FEELING RESTRICTED
OR BURDENED BY ONE ANOTHER.

THERE ARE MANY DIFFERENT TYPES OF MARITAL AND non-marital romantic relationships in this world, but not all are created equally. Generally, there is no such thing as an easy relationship; they will always require consistency and work on both parts.

Some people are just looking for companionship, and others want to find their true love. There's a huge difference between simply being friends with benefits versus getting married.

Relationships are hard work on any level; there will be good times and bad. If you're up for the challenge then there are a few things to keep in mind:

• Talk about feelings, goals, expectations, and desires early on in the relationship so that you don't end up expecting something different from what your partner is willing to give. Honesty at all costs.

• Find a way to continuously challenge each other while still maintaining a healthy flow.

• Work on yourselves individually and as a couple.

• Learn what the boundaries are for both of you so that they aren't constantly being tested. Boundaries will help maintain respect in any relationship.

It's important to have boundaries with those you love, and it can be challenging when people overstep their bounds.

Boundaries offer a sense of security for both you and your partner. They can give each of you the freedom to be yourselves without feeling restricted or burdened by one another. Boundaries are also important for setting expectations and establishing a proper balance in the relationship.

There are many ways that people handle healthy boundaries, but they all have certain things in common:

- Helpful boundaries are always specific. They're based on your needs and values, not anyone else's.
- You should be able to say no when you need to.
- There is no expectation of an inordinate amount of time or energy investment from either partner.
- Boundaries are ongoing and open for discussion as needed. They're not set in stone, but a sense of respect is always necessary.

Boundaries exist on an individual level with other people and within yourself; they don't just have to be limited to your relationship. There are many different ways that people can handle healthy boundaries in a relationship—here's just one example: If one partner can't make decisions on their own because of feeling insecure about themselves, they need to have an open dialogue and discuss how the other person is able to handle this.

It can be helpful for partners who have opposing wants and needs in a relationship to take turns, because that way it isn't just one person always accommodating the other.

It can also be beneficial for a person who often feels like they're being taken advantage of by other people, but doesn't feel fulfilled in their relationship, to create specific limits on what they're willing to do.

When you don't have any boundaries, it can create some serious issues. Here are a few examples:

• It's difficult when one partner is always giving and never getting anything back in return.

• It can be hurtful when one partner is always making decisions for the other without seeking input first.

• One person may feel like they're being taken advantage of, while the other feels resentment because their needs are never met. The relationship might start to deteriorate, and it's hard to repair once this happens.

If you find yourself feeling disconnected or frustrated by your partner, take a moment to consider the possibility that you might need to set some boundaries. When you're in the right space, it should feel good and satisfying—not angering or burdening.

Setting healthy boundaries is a sign of personal strength because it's admitting that you deserve love too.

In a healthy relationship, partners should be able to say no when they need to and set the parameters of their time investment. However, they should also know where all those boundaries are in advance so the other isn't continuously being told no over and over because they continually get shot down for crossing boundaries they didn't know existed.

Remember my story about Danny from earlier? Because there were no consistent boundaries, he had to frequently tell me no—but I never knew when it would be OK to try to touch him or show affection because his response was inconsistent. Sometimes it was fine and sometimes it wasn't. There were even times we would be in the middle of some sort of intimate embrace and he would suddenly push me away without warning.

Learning when and how to enforce them is every bit as important for a relationship as having them in the first place.

*Special Note on Sexual Boundaries...

In pretty much all romantic relationships, sex comes into play. This could be a whole book on it's own (which I may write in the future), but I will touch on the subject now.

FINDING YOUR BOUNDARY LINES—HOW TO DISCOVER YOUR SEXUAL LIMITS AND STICK TO THEM

When it comes to emotional and sexual boundaries, it can be tempting to formulate a fixed set of ideas of what they "should" be rather than looking more closely at what works best for us personally. Our boundaries are entirely unique to us, and it's important to recognize that what works for your best friend might be entirely uncomfortable for you—and vice versa.

There are different aspects of boundary building to consider as we grow and evolve. Particularly in a sexual context, our personal preferences may significantly alter as we mature and come to know ourselves more consciously.

Unsure how to find your safety lines? Start by listening to your gut while developing enough confidence to be able to say no to what (and who) isn't a good fit.

So—how do we go about establishing our ground rules? Here are some key fundamentals:

Listen to your gut. Learning to tune in to your personal intuition is crucial to your emotional well-being. If you notice you are feeling agitated or compromised within a situation, then it's time to take a step back. You might be temporarily overwhelmed, and a few moments alone will help you realize you're OK. Or this could be your gut telling you that a line has been crossed.

Reflect to progress. How we feel after being sexually experimental with someone can help us realize if this is something we truly enjoy, or simply an act we are agreeing in order to please the person we are attracted to. Meditation, journaling, or even talking to a trusted friend can help us process our thoughts to clarify those all-important boundaries.

It's good to talk. If you are with someone who respects you, then you should be able to speak freely to them about your boundaries. Practice regular positive communication about how you are feeling and thinking about your relationship or shared situation. The right person will appreciate your honesty and work with you to explore your limits without pushing them too far.

You are a worthy individual who deserves to have their boundaries respected. We develop our ideas of "right and wrong" all the way from childhood. They are influenced by the people we go on to meet, the experiences we have had, and the principles we have developed. Not everyone will agree with you, but this doesn't mean you (or they) are "wrong." What is important is that your safety lines remain protected and respected.

Your boundaries may change as you get to know someone. Your limits of physical contact, for example, might alter as you begin to trust someone and allow them a little closer. This is a natural part of developing a healthy structure between you and another person. Every relationship will feel a little different. Travel gently—keeping your emotional health a priority at all times!

FOOD FOR THOUGHT

- Know what you're comfortable with, and don't be afraid to say it, even if that means someone might get mad or upset in the process.
- Remember that you are the only person who has your best interests in mind 100 percent of the time.
- When it comes to emotional and sexual boundaries, it can be tempting to formulate a fixed set of ideas of what they "should" be rather than looking more closely at what works best for us personally.
- Boundaries are always open to discussion if problems arise. It's not about black or white but finding the right balance.
- Also, remember that boundaries are going to change and evolve as you grow. This is a natural part of developing a healthy structure between you and another person.

In the next chapter, we will discuss the importance of setting healthy boundaries at work. Boundaries exist on an individual level, and they don't just have to be limited to a relationship.

AT WORK

USING HEALTHY BOUNDARIES AT WORK IS GOOD FOR YOUR HEALTH. CREATING BOUNDARIES MEANS TAKING CHARGE OF YOUR WORK WORLD AND CREATING SPACE FOR YOURSELF. YOU'LL FEEL LESS STRESSED, LESS BACKED UP, AND MORE BALANCED.

DEPENDING ON THE KIND OF WORK YOU DO, KEEPING boundaries in the workplace can be difficult, because it's also usually a place where you spend many hours each week, and the relationships are oftentimes more intense and personal than those outside of work. Boundaries at work also need to include physical space as well—for example, people should not eat lunch at their desks or talk on the phone while walking around if these things are not permitted or if they distract others.

There are also emotional boundaries that need to be kept in place for a healthy work environment. This includes not talking about personal issues with coworkers and needing to have "off-limits" topics when interacting with them, like family problems, financial worries, medical conditions, and more sensitive subjects.

By following these guidelines, you can maintain healthy boundaries at work and create a safe space for everyone.

WHAT HAPPENS IF YOU DON'T KEEP BOUNDARIES?

If physical or emotional boundaries are not maintained in the workplace, it will eventually impact your health and productivity. For example, if someone doesn't have time to take a lunch break, they might start to feel anxiety or stress. That can lead to much more serious health issues down the road.

Additionally, if you are constantly talking about personal issues with coworkers and colleagues, it can cause tension at work that may then lead to conflict elsewhere.

Also, depending on your position in a company, boundaries can vary. For instance, if you own or run a small agency, boundaries will need to be utilized every day. If you have an assistant, they may know your work schedule and personal life better than anyone else. For example, they may know the last time you left work and when your partner is coming by to pick up some dry cleaning.

If you are expected to do the work of three dozen people and feel overwhelmed with projects, chances are you're not good at delegating. Fortunately, this is a skill that can be developed. Let go of your tasks sometimes; trust team members and play to their strengths.

No matter your position or line of work, there are some tips that can help.

DEVELOP A SYSTEM

David Allen, an expert on productivity and author of *Getting Things Done: The Art of Stress-Free Productivity*, suggests that tasks should be sorted into one of four categories:

• Do it

• Defer it

• Delegate it

• Drop it

Address an issue only once before moving on.

If you find yourself in the middle of long, drawn-out interactions, creating structure can help. Doing this ensures that everyone will share input about the project and puts you in control of what information to cover before embarking on the project itself.

You can also create structure where there was none before. You could meet weekly instead of a lackadaisical visit to your office from your co-worker here and there. That way, you both know what's going on in the company and there will be a more structured relationship. You might consider asking your boss (or employee) what he or she expects from you and what you might expect from him or her.

Also, avoid gossiping. People who may not even be in the loop can find out information that they then gossip about. Don't be the person parked in the parking lot of the bar, catching up and/or talking smack.

Be careful about privacy in an office environment. If you have private information, you shouldn't be sharing it with everyone. Be especially cautious about this in small offices where it's important to ask permission before sharing information with others. In addition, keep any private information you learn during the course of your work relationship to yourself. This includes financial records, customer accounts, contracts, and any other pertinent information you come across.

Using healthy boundaries at work is good for your health. Creating boundaries means taking charge of your work world and creating space for yourself. You'll feel less stressed, less backed up, and more balanced.

FOOD FOR THOUGHT

- Create a system for your tasks.
- Don't gossip about people.
- Avoid sharing private information with others, including financial records or customer accounts you come across in the course of doing your work (unless it's pertinent to what they're working on).
- Take breaks or you might start to feel anxiety or stress.
- Don't talk about personal issues with coworkers and colleagues.
- Depending on your position, boundaries will need to be utilized every day.
- Delegate. Let go of your tasks sometimes; trust team members and play to their strengths.

In conclusion, remember that boundaries are good for your health. Create space by setting limits and deciding what you want to do with tasks, information, or work-related documents as they come up in the course of doing your job.

And that's all fine and good for work, but what about at home, you may ask?

AT HOME

> YOUR BOUNDARIES ARE *YOURS;* DO WHAT FEELS RIGHT. BUT BE SURE TO PAY ATTENTION TO THE BOUNDARIES OF OTHERS AS WELL.

WHEN IT COMES TO MAINTAINING HEALTHY boundaries in your own home, it's best to start with the little things and work your way up. This is because everyone in the home is likely already used to everything being a certain way.

To maintain your own sense of dignity, make sure you are able to control your personal space in ways such as going to bed when you want or closing a door if someone is too close for comfort.

When it comes to **chores,** find balance between what you can and cannot do, but make sure to keep the responsibilities you are responsible for as your own.

For **finances**, be aware of who earns what in terms of income coming into the household so that bills can be paid on time once they come due.

The best way to maintain boundaries with **children** is by showing them how to maintain boundaries with others. Show your children how you would like them to treat other people by treating relatives accordingly in the same way that you want their friends treated. This includes showing respect for parents and grandparents while also listening when adults are talking so as not to interrupt or get distracted. Be aware of how your children are treating their friends and help them learn that it is important to respect everyone for who they are.

There is no "set number" on what constitutes a healthy distance for **physical intimacy**, but the best way to figure it out is by learning your own preferences and then talking with other people about theirs as well so you can figure out how to determine your own.

When it comes to **social media,** it's best to establish boundaries ahead of time so that everyone knows what is expected and where the lines are drawn.

It can be difficult for those who were not raised in a home with healthy boundaries from the beginning. For these people, they may have moved between multiple caregivers throughout their childhood, or had a lot of siblings, which makes establishing personal space and boundaries difficult.

For those who were raised in a home with less than healthy boundaries, it can be harder to learn how to establish them on their own so that they can avoid repeating the cycle of unhealthy relationships and abuse when they have children themselves or interact with other adults. This is not an easy process, but it begins by learning to set boundaries for themselves and then learning how to respect other people's needs, wants, and opinions.

When establishing this in your own home, the best course of action is a balance between giving in while also maintaining personal responsibility. If you always give in when someone asks for something that they don't really need, you will find yourself quickly running out of money and feeling resentful. If you just keep saying yes to avoid dealing with your own needs or emotions in any way, then it is possible that those feelings might build up until they become overwhelming and lead to a breakdown.

The best advice I can give here is to **find a balance between what you can and cannot do**. That way, when it comes time for chores, one person will always be responsible while the other helps out with tasks that they are capable of doing or helping with as well. When it comes to finances, both partners should have access to all financial information so that one person doesn't have to take on the responsibility of paying all bills.

Children are taught best by example and need to see their parents setting boundaries. That way, they learn first without having them enforced against them with harsh consequences when they step outside these boundaries, such as grounding or taking away things that they enjoy. It's important for kids from a young age to understand the consequences of breaking the rules in order to learn right from wrong, but they also need to watch adults model good behavior and respect between each other.

PARENTS WHO OVERSTEP THEIR BOUNDARIES

Parents who overstep their boundaries can cause a lot of problems for the children. They may tell them what to do or not let them make decisions on their own, even when they are an adult.

What do healthy boundaries between parents and children look like?

• Honesty and respect.

• Picking boundaries that are clear for the whole family to work around.

• Learning how to apologize and work through any conflicts in a healthy way.

• Keeping the lines of communication open. This means making sure everyone has someone they feel safe talking with about their feelings or ideas, even if it's not the same person every time.

• Coming to an understanding of what is most valuable for everyone in your family.

• It's important to be able to trust each other and know that you can count on someone when needed. If this doesn't feel like it's possible, then they might not be respecting your boundaries enough.

You deserve peace and respect in your life. Everyone does. Thus includes everyone else in your home.

Your boundaries are *yours;* do what feels right. But be sure to pay attention to the boundaries of others as well.

If you're experiencing family members who overstep boundaries, it's good to talk with them about how they make you feel. Communicating the issue will let them know what has happened and allow for change in their behavior. If the conversation isn't going well then it may be a sign of an unhealthy relationship, which can lead to a lot of problems in the future.

*SPECIAL NOTE TO THE CHILDREN (GROWN OR NOT). Parents who overstep their boundaries are not only hurting you but also your child (or future child) if you are also a parent, so it's important that they know what is and isn't appropriate behavior. If this continues, then there may be some kind of abuse that will need intervention from professionals or law enforcement agencies.

Boundaries set for yourself and your children will allow for a healthy relationship with both. It's important that the family unit is respected by everyone in it, so if boundaries aren't being set then you need to figure out why or how to enforce them.

BOUNDARIES FOR CHILDREN

There is a downside to letting children share in decision-making. Offering them too much power and control can be stressful for the parent, even if it's just a small amount of control. This causes parenting to be ineffective. The only way for parents' power and control over children to work is when they have established limits and boundaries.

Being a parent and friend at the same time is difficult. Parents must set limits for their children, which may be unpopular.

Setting boundaries for children ensures that they feel safe and comfortable in a world of structure. When someone is unhappy or uncomfortable, it takes a toll on their wellness and growth—an aspect that poses an extreme disadvantage to some parents who lack the experience or ability to establish such boundaries for example.

One benefit of parents setting limits with their kids is that the child will be able to set their own limits as they mature.

Too much flexibility in parenting means children will have too much control and power. This may indicate a family is experiencing a crisis.

Even when a child's behavior doesn't reach the level of problematic, too much autonomy can result in an increased risk of irresponsible behaviors from the child. Conversely, excessively restrictive parenting can lead to extreme rebellious behaviors as the adolescent starts stepping out of their dependent phase.

In order to set boundaries for children, parents need to be clear with their expectations. It also helps if the child is in tune with their parent's expectations as well and not just given arbitrary rules on a whim. This will ensure that they're able to understand why you established certain limits and help them make better choices.

When setting rules for your children, find out what they want and need so you can have a baseline of understanding between the two parties involved. If you're not sure how to answer that question, then asking them "What do you think?" will help clear things up quickly. Children often don't know their own limitations and have trouble setting limits for themselves, so help them understand what is and isn't OK.

Set expectations before a situation arises instead of reacting in the heat of the moment. The later you establish boundaries with your children, the more likely they will be able to disregard those requests as arbitrary commands rather than a request for cooperation.

FOOD FOR THOUGHT

- Be honest with yourself and your kids.
- Don't be afraid of the truth; admit when you're wrong or know what is best for our children.
- Don't wait for a crisis to establish rules—set the limits first.
- Give your children power over their choices without giving them too much control or responsibility—this also helps them learn how to make good decisions as well.
- Find out what your child wants so you know where they're coming from, then reach a compromise.

- Ask your child for their ideas when establishing rules to make them feel involved in the process and also get a sense of what they're comfortable with doing themselves—this will help set good boundaries later on that are manageable for both parties.

BOUNDARIES ARE NOT MEANT TO MAKE YOU FEEL LIKE A VICTIM, THEY'RE MEANT FOR YOUR PROTECTION.

People must understand why setting personal boundaries is important before it can be enforced. Next, we will explore the further reach of family boundaries not just within the home, but also with extended family as well as friends.

WITH FAMILY & FRIENDS

REMEMBER THAT BOUNDARIES DO NOT HAVE
TO BE SET IN STONE, AND THEY CAN ALWAYS
CHANGE AS TIME GOES ON—AS LONG AS THE
LINES OF COMMUNICATION REMAIN OPEN.

ASIDE FROM JUST THE PARENT-CHILD RELATIONSHIP, boundaries may need to come in to play with other family members and friendships. It is difficult to set boundaries with family members, as oftentimes they have known each other for a long time and the relationships are very complicated. Or the need to establish healthy boundaries may be linked to an adult needing more independence from their parents or siblings.

There can also come a point where your friend's behavior has become too much of an issue to be able to continue the friendship. Set boundaries with friends if you do not feel accepted or appreciated, as that will only lead to negative feelings and resentment on your part.

Boundary issues can come up with siblings (either adult or child), grandparents, cousins, aunts and uncles, you name it. This occurs most often when you have differing belief systems from your friends and family. For example, if you are a vegan and your family is not, it can be difficult to continue spending time with them knowing that they don't share the same views as you. In this case, setting boundaries would mean limiting or eliminating contact with those friends/family members until such time as there may be a chance for more understanding between both parties. This is especially pertinent when it comes to religious or political views. When these subjects come up a lot, gatherings can just get downright awkward.

Boundary issues with friends can occur when you feel as though your friend's behavior is unacceptable, or vice versa. Sometimes this may be a one-time incident, while other times it could be something that happens repeatedly over time (beware if the frequency of unpleasant behaviors outweighs the enjoyable interactions). If these boundaries are not established and maintained, then the friendship could eventually become unhealthy or even detrimental. It may be helpful to discuss the situation with your friend and come up with a plan that works for both of you.

Boundary issues are difficult in any relationship; however, they are necessary if we want our relationships to grow and flourish rather than stagnate or become "toxic" (although I am not a fan of that word because it implies so much judgment).

Remember that boundaries do not have to be set in stone, and they can always change as time goes on—as long as the lines of communication remain open. Setting healthy boundaries is a way of maintaining our self-respect and ensuring we are being treated the way we want (and deserve) to be treated by others.

With family members or friends with whom you disagree about something, it can be difficult to know where the boundaries are. However, you should always respect yourself and your opinions, thoughts, and beliefs in order to maintain a healthy relationship with these people moving forward.

As far as setting up boundaries when it comes to family members or friends who don't respect your choices (i.e., if they try to make you feel guilty for not going to church), understand the line between acceptance and manipulation. If they are trying to manipulate or guilt-trip you, then this is a problem. The best thing to do in these situations would be to tell them how their behavior makes you feel (i.e., hurt; disrespected) and to then tell them how you would like for them to treat you.

Setting boundaries with family members and friends is difficult, but it can be done if the need arises. If these individuals refuse to respect your boundaries, it may mean that they do not value your feelings/opinions enough to want healthy relationships with you. In this situation, it may be time to re-evaluate the relationship and whether or not you want to continue maintaining ties with these people in your life

FOOD FOR THOUGHT

- Boundaries may need to come into play with other friends and family members.
- Setting boundaries among friends and family can be tricky because oftentimes you have known each other for a long time.
- Family boundaries may be linked to an adult needing more independence from their parents or siblings.
- There can also come a point where your friend's behavior has become too much of an issue if you do not feel accepted, appreciated, etc.

Setting boundaries in your relationships with friends, family members, and other people is important for maintaining healthy relationships. It's not always easy these days to know who you can trust or how to deal with the issues that come up when it comes to disagreements about religion, politics, etc. Boundaries are difficult but necessary if we want our relationships to grow and flourish rather than stagnate. This is a way of maintaining our self-respect and ensuring we are being treated the way we want (and deserve) by others.

And yes, this chapter applies to in-person interactions, but what about the growing popularity of interacting with our loved ones (and not-so-loved ones) in cyberspace?

ONLINE

IT IS UP TO YOU TO DECIDE WHO DESERVES SPACE IN YOUR LIFE.

SETTING BOUNDARIES ONLINE IS A NECESSITY FOR ALL of us. It's not just about keeping an eye on your kids, it's also about protecting yourself and those around you from cyberbullying, cyberstalking, or other dangers that lurk in cyberspace—even just annoying drama. With the right precautions in place, we can have the freedom of being connected without having to worry so much about what could happen if our guard is down.

Limits such as:

• How often and with how many people children chat online.

• Keeping track of all the known passwords.

• Monitoring kids' usernames—and change them when necessary, requiring a form of identification.

• Establishing age restrictions for certain types of media exposure (age-inappropriate websites) and everyday activities (complex interactions).

• Practicing good digital hygiene skills to better protect family members' private information.

The best way to set boundaries for your own protection is to make sure that you are careful about the things you do online and take appropriate measures.

Social Media

This is a pretty big tent to cover because there are so many variables. Here are some to consider:

1) Limiting scrolling time

2) Resisting the need to argue or "poke the bear"

3) Setting certain posts to a limited audience

4) Assessing whether you should post a controversial topic before doing it. What will it achieve?

5) Responding to messages

6) Deleting comments and posts

7) Posting appropriate photos and personal details

8) "Vaugebooking" (I will explain this)

9) Oversharing and attention-seeking "diary posts"

Sooooo, yeah... there is a lot to think about. Let's tackle these one at a time.

LIMIT SCROLLING TIME

We all *need* to set boundaries on scrolling social media. We won't know what will happen if we don't have a limit.

Set space for yourself and your own feelings; it can be a healthy habit to take breaks from scrolling all the time. It is addictive and even leads to serious self-esteem issues. Nothing good comes from constantly comparing ourselves to others.

RESIST THE NEED TO ARGUE OR "POKE THE BEAR"

This is a term used online when someone wants an argument. It refers to poking at something that makes someone angry and "wakes the bear" (aka the person's temper). A good rule of thumb, if you don't want to have an argument—do not poke! When people start arguing on social media, they lose sight of their real life and the way it works. Stick close to your guns, even if someone is trying to poke at you.

To avoid argument, do not go poking around for one! You will get lost in the conversation and forget what you are really doing.

Stay strong even if someone tries to poke at you on social media. You should not let them change your opinion about things or make up a story for themselves.

SETTING CERTAIN POSTS TO A LIMITED AUDIENCE

Not everything we do needs to be public. It's fine to keep some things private when we post them on social media.

You can set your profile so not everything you do publicly shows up online, which will protect your privacy in ways and let others know it isn't always okay to share.

Some people set up a secondary account for the posts they don't want everyone to see, which gives them more control over their privacy and who can follow them.

ASSESS WHETHER YOU SHOULD POST A CONTROVERSIAL TOPIC BEFORE DOING IT

If we really think about what we are going to post, it can save us from a lot of trouble.

Assess whether you really want to say what you're about to say before posting it! Seriously, think things over rather than just writing off the first impulse as the only one worth taking.

Consider if saying something controversial is going to get you the reaction you want. If it's not, then maybe don't post it. It will save you from a lot of trouble in the future. Thoughtlessly posting can be very dangerous without thinking things through clearly ahead of time.

RESPONDING TO MESSAGES AND COMMENTS

It's easy to get caught up in a conversation. But we need to set boundaries and respond when it is appropriate.

Don't forget about how you might make someone feel by ignoring the messages—this can lead to an unhealthy disconnection with life, friends, and people we love. But still, even though it is rude not to reply, sometimes it is easy to get lost in the onslaught of messages.

Make sure to respond when it is appropriate, especially if someone is trying to get in touch with you. Make sure you pay attention to the messages that matter and ignore the ones that don't so you can stay focused.

It is up to you to decide who deserves space in your life. Even though it is easy to get lost in your inbox sometimes, make sure you remember how *they* feel.

Doing this will save us in the long run.

We will be able to use these skills with confidence when we need them in real life. Remembering how to deal with people online takes a bit of practice. It may not seem like a lot, but this can really help us grow in our real-life interactions.

DELETING COMMENTS AND POSTS

When someone leaves a comment or post that makes us feel uncomfortable, it's OK to delete it.

It can be hard to ignore people online when they are trying to get our attention in a negative way, but we need to do this for ourselves if they continue. It's better to ignore them completely instead of getting into an argument because then we are giving them more attention than they deserve.

It can be hard when people try and get in touch with you in an aggressive way on social media, but doing this for ourselves can help us maintain our self-respect. Just ignore them completely instead of giving in to what they want from us because that will make things worse.

POST ONLY APPROPRIATE PHOTOS AND PERSONAL DETAILS

I can't stress this enough: *think twice (or thrice) about what you post online.*

Make sure that when you post photos or personal information, it's something that represents you well and doesn't give away too much of your identity or personal life. There is no need to put out every detail for someone else to see. Some may have very different intentions for this type of content.

When we post photos or personal information, it should represent us well while keeping certain details private so other people don't find out who you are.

Despite this, many will do this anyway. But policing others won't help the matter either. It can be hard not to get involved when a friend or family member posts inappropriate photos or personal information, but calling someone out publicly is never helpful. How do you feel when others try to "correct" you in front of everyone? It sucks.

"VAUGEBOOKING"

This is when you write vaguely about a topic on Facebook or Instagram so people will not know what is going on with your life. It can be irritating to see these posts, though the person usually has their reasons (no matter how asinine) for keeping certain things private.

Even though it can be annoying to see "vaguebooking" posts, and it seems they are trying to avoid letting people in on what is going on with their life, it is usually done by someone who wants attention or pity. Being cryptic will usually get lots of people asking questions about "what's wrong?" or "what happened!?" and give the person posting plenty of opportunity to talk about themselves and their problem openly while still appearing like they had intended to keep it private.

And it's annoying AF.

If you are guilty of this, I suggest you reassess why you do it. And then cut it out. I unfollow those who do this a lot, and so do a lot of other people. All it accomplishes is stirring up a bunch of drama. And it only attracts into your social circle those who thrive on drama.

If you want to avoid drama (for real), then don't create or engage with these kinds of posts. End of story.

OVERSHARING AND ATTENTION-SEEKING "DIARY POSTS"

As I just mentioned above, we need to think twice before we post something online.

When it comes to "oversharing" on social media or indulging in attention-seeking posts, there is a line between not giving away too much of your personal life and keeping your friends in the loop. It's good that people share their lives with others, but sometimes they can go too far with these types of posts and give away too much information.

Think about it: does your mother-in-law really need to know about your husband's habit of clogging the toilet with used condoms? (Not kidding—I actually saw someone post about this.)

And do you really believe someone wants to read your daily thousand-word tirades about everything going on in your life?

Let's think... NO.

That is all.

THE SOCIAL MEDIA DOPAMINE HIGH

While we are constantly on our phones or computers, scrolling through the latest updates and seeing how many likes/comments we have gotten recently can actually cause a dopamine high. It feels good to get attention from others, but don't let that feeling take control of your life. We need to make sure social media doesn't become more important than the people and things in our real lives.

When it comes to social media, understand that getting attention from others can feel good for a moment but should not take priority over anything else in life. If you find yourself constantly scrolling through your newsfeed or giving out comments on posts more than spending time with friends/family, then maybe it's time to put down the phone and turn off notifications for a while.

FOOD FOR THOUGHT

- Set boundaries for how long you spend looking at social media so that you don't get too addicted or feel bad about yourself.
- Find a digital detox buddy or group! It will help you stay accountable. You can share tips on how to do it successfully with each other, too.
- Try using a social media "cleanse" app like the Unplug App or Moment—these apps can help you take control of how much time you spend scrolling through updates when it comes to certain apps, if that is what's causing problems for you.
- If all else fails, delete some of your accounts, if possible (starting with the ones taking up too much time).
- Remember: social media isn't real life. Don't let it become more important than your physical relationships!
- And if you are really struggling with these issues, talk to a therapist or counselor. It is super important to get support and help from others when we need it the most. Social media addiction is a legit problem.

The key to social media is setting boundaries on what you post and when. Our lives are not defined by the things we put online.

No one has a perfect life, even if they make their life look perfect on social media. Protect your self-esteem from the pressure of always searching for it online because no one has a perfect life, even if enough filters make it seem like it is flawless. Remind yourself that you are special and your feelings matter regardless of what other people do on social media.

Stop caring about what everyone else is doing online and remember that we are all human. Social media can only make us feel so good if it's not real life, which makes up for the great things in our lives.

YOU are what is most important, and this brings me to our final chapter.

YOURSELF

WHEN IT COMES DOWN TO IT, A PERSON WITH HEALTHY BOUNDARIES HAS LEARNED THEIR WANTS AND NEEDS AS WELL AS THE REASONS FOR CREATING THEM—THEY CAN CONFIDENTLY SAY NOW: "THIS IS WHO I AM."

HAVING BOUNDARIES WITH YOURSELF MEANS NOT being afraid to do things that are different or outside of the norm in order for you to be true to who you really are.

I always said to myself that I would never live my life for what other people wanted me to be.

But then I realized that I was doing just that.

The day when people finally respected my boundaries changed everything for me. It was then that I started to find myself again and start living the life I wanted to live.

I can confidently say now with 100 percent certainty: "This is who I am. And I am proud to be me."

But, holy crabcakes, it took me a while to get there.

Many people struggle with healthy boundaries. It can be difficult to live without fear of what other people might think—because the constant need for approval and fear of rejection is all-consuming. When living in a world that seems bent on compromising strong personal boundaries, many find it hard to speak up when someone does something they're not OK with or even recognize their own personal boundaries.

But there are ways to develop strong boundaries, and it starts with understanding the reasons for them; what they look like in reality and how you can create them. It's important to know your wants and needs as well—this will help when discussing your boundaries with others. And always remember: a person who has healthy boundaries is able to refuse when others push too hard.

When it comes down to it, a person with healthy boundaries has learned their wants and needs as well as the reasons for creating them—they can confidently say now: "This is who I am." And that's all you need to be proud of yourself, too. Living this way will allow you to live with your head held high, and that's worth it.

There are many reasons why people have boundaries, but for the purposes of this book, we've covered what healthy boundaries look like in a world gone too far. When it comes to having boundaries with yourself, the first thing one must do is know your own wants and needs—these should be discussed with others as well. It is crucial to know what your boundaries are because when it comes down to it, a person with healthy boundaries doesn't even have to set them anymore.

Why does it seem like the world is always trying to compromise our boundaries? Perhaps it's because people don't know what they want, what they need, or even their own boundaries.

IT IS CRUCIAL TO KNOW WHAT YOUR BOUND-ARIES ARE BECAUSE WHEN IT COMES DOWN TO IT, A PERSON WITH HEALTHY BOUND-ARIES DOESN'T EVEN HAVE TO SET THEM ANYMORE.

When you learn your wants and needs as well as the reasons for creating them, a person will be confident in who they are and what they need. And that alone should be enough to give anyone pride of self. You're not living someone else's life anymore—live the one you want to.

Boundaries can help us find that inner peace that we might have otherwise lost. Once these are set, it will be easier to say no when necessary—but always with the knowledge of why you were doing so. A person who has healthy boundaries knows their own opinions, does not bargain or compromise values for others, and has learned the wants and needs of themselves.

WHEN WE LET OURSELVES FEEL VICTIMIZED THOUGH, WE GIVE OUR POWER AWAY. AND THAT STUNTS OUR PROGRESS AS HUMAN BEINGS.

For years, I pitied myself in silence because of my lack of self-esteem. Other people always seemed more important than me—even if they weren't actually doing anything for themselves or those around them.

I started to find myself again and start living the life I wanted to live. What helped the most was knowing my personal boundaries.

I grew up as a shy girl in school, and it only seemed to intensify in college when I started meeting people on campus. People constantly wanted something from me (or so I felt at the time), but I didn't want anything from them—at least not anything they were willing to give.

It took time for me to learn my boundaries—what I wanted and needed from others and vice versa.

I became confident in knowing who I am, and that's given me the strength to say no when someone asks something of me that violates those boundaries or doesn't align with them. It has also helped immensely in being able to tell people how their actions make me feel because now I know I don't have to experience their consequences.

I'll never forget what helped me the most—learning that when we let ourselves feel victimized, we give our power away. And that stunts our progress as human beings.

Boundaries can be difficult because some people want you to give in or compromise your values when they ask something of you—it's like they're robbing you of your power. It can be hard to look at yourself and recognize that you're worth something, but once you do, everything will change for the better.

I've learned so much about myself in this past decade by implementing boundaries into my life. I know now what I want, need, or am willing to give.

I was in a relationship for about a year where my partner continuously pushed me to compromise, and I always felt victimized because of it—but now that I know what's important to me, we are both happier people (although we are no longer a couple, and that's perfectly OK).

Boundaries can help everyone find their inner peace by understanding themselves and how they want things done or handled. It's time we start talking about boundaries and embrace them as a way to find ourselves.

I don't know what life would have been like if I had never learned healthy boundaries, but I do know that it has changed my perspective on how people interact with me. You can be assertive without being aggressive when you establish your personal boundaries—all it takes is practicing a little more self-control.

It took a long time for me, but today, this introverted girl has found her voice...and she's not afraid to use it (although some might say I *overuse* it).

I want you to feel empowered by this book because it will help you learn how set healthy boundaries as well as understand why these boundaries are so important for your health, mental state, physical safety, and relationships in the future.

I have a lot more self-respect now than before, and with boundaries in place, no one will ever be able to take advantage of me again.

Because *we* choose whether or not we are taken advantage of.

Picture it: What would happen if you let your guard down? What if your need for boundaries completely dissipates? And they just fall into place naturally because you are so confident in who you are? What could that mean for the future of your relationships with others?

There will always be relationships that hurt us, but we have the power of choice on who crosses our personal boundary line or not.

INSTILLING CONSEQUENCES

In this final chapter, I want to go over some of the different types and consequences for when boundaries are crossed.

Boundaries can be broken by people who feel they have a right to take what doesn't belong to them: possessions, emotions, or time—even if they don't mean any harm.

TYPES OF BOUNDARIES: PHYSICAL, EMOTIONAL, MENTAL.

- An **emotional boundary** is the most important because you're allowing yourself to be vulnerable, and people can take advantage of that.
- **Mental**: asking for help from others but not letting them control your life or make decisions for you.
- **Physical:** don't let anyone touch you without consent.

What should you do when someone violates your personal boundaries?

First, come to understand what happened. How did the person cross your line? Were they being disrespectful or abusive?

Then you should address how this makes you feel and talk about why. You'll also need to enforce consequences if they don't stop right away (i.e.; walk away or cancel upcoming plans with them).

If someone crosses your boundary on an emotional level (i.e., breaks your trust or hurts your feelings), try not to take this personally or feel hurt by the person as much as possible. You should allow yourself to be vulnerable and express how that makes you feel in order to maintain boundaries with them moving forward.

When someone has broken your emotional boundaries, help them understand how this makes you feel and talk about why that is not OK with you. They will likely need to apologize for breaking the trust or respect between both of you in order fix it.

If someone crosses your boundary on a mental level (i.e., manipulating or gaslighting), understand what the person is trying to say, then come up with boundaries that work for both of you. This way, neither party feels taken advantage of or hurt by the other.

When someone has broken your mental boundaries, again try not to take this personally or feel hurt by the person as much as possible. Sometimes a compromise is needed in order for both of you to be happy with the relationship moving forward.

When someone crosses a boundary on a physical level (i.e., violates your personal space), talk to them about their behavior and let them know it's not cool, then enforce any consequences that might need to be set in place (i.e., pull back or, in more serious situations, threaten to call the police).

Know that it is never your fault when someone violates you physically. You deserve respect.

When people are crossing your physical space (i.e., touching you without permission), speak up for yourself and let them know that their behavior is not OK with you. If someone continues to cross your boundaries after this point, get away and bring it to someone's attention.

Finally, some examples of healthy personal boundaries, for yourself and others to consider, include:

- Being able to say no without feeling guilty or obligated (e.g., if you don't want to do something, it doesn't matter the reason).
- Time management (e.g., spend time with people who make you happy instead of those who only show up when they need something from you).
- Financial support (e.g., if someone asks for money, it's time to tell them no).
- Physical touch (e.g., if someone touches you without your consent, say something and get away from that person as soon as possible).
- Privacy (e.g., someone looking through your closet or journal).

When it comes down to it, don't let people take advantage of you, physically or emotionally. Period. If someone is taking your things without asking, and it's not a shared item like milk in the fridge, they are violating your personal space and need to be told so.

There are many ways people can cross our boundary lines. It is crucial that if someone does something that makes you feel uncomfortable, you speak up and let them know. If we let things slide and don't speak up about what happened, then there might be a chance for someone else to take advantage of us as well in the future, or for that person to overstep someone else's bounds who won't react as rationally.

Because everyone is different, there are many different parts of this book that might resonate with you while they don't for someone else and vice versa.

Personal boundaries are just that: *personal.*

With all that being said, I will conclude with some final words that are applicable for everyone...

CONCLUSION...

Don't Be A Boundary Whore!

So, what have we learned?

We've discussed the problems with boundary whoring and how it builds walls you may find yourself trapped in. We've also talked about what boundaries are and why they're important to establish in your relationships. There were even more things mentioned that I didn't get into; like where to draw the line between being a bad bitch and having boundaries. ;)

The goal of this book was not only to help you figure out whether or not you are being a pushover or boundary whoring, but also give some insight on how to avoid unneeded conflict in your future relationships/interactions.

Finally, I want everyone reading this to know that my intention for writing about something like this is not to make you feel bad or like I'm some all-knowing expert on relationships (even though I do have a pretty long list of credentials). My goal for writing about boundaries (and boundary whoring) has nothing at all to do with my desire to control your actions, but rather it stems from a sincere interest in seeing everyone have positive interactions in their lives. In the end, I hope that after reading this you will have a better understanding of boundaries and how they play into your life.

If there is anything that I've learned about boundaries, it's this: we need them to meet our needs for safety, security, stability, hope—without which no sane person would ever take another risk in human interaction. And just as importantly (if not more so), we need boundaries to meet our needs for intimacy, connection, and affection—which is what makes life work.

Boundaries are a bitch? Well...yeah. Sometimes they can be, but in the end it's all worth it once you figure out how to balance things out with people who make your life better instead of worse.

That's all I got for now. But I will be back with more in future books to help you live your own unedited life!

Enjoyed this book? Don't forget to leave a review!
Every review matters, and it matters a *lot!*
Head over to Amazon or wherever you purchased this
book to leave an honest review for me.
I thank you endlessly.

ABOUT THE AUTHOR

Qatarina Wanders is a former circus performer turned author and self-made businesswoman (with a wee bit of a unicorn obsession). In addition, she is a single mom, competitive weightlifter, avid reader, and skydiver.

She built her book-production business, Wandering Words Media, in 2016 when she decided it was time to settle down from traveling circus life and build something more sustainable.

After a ton of trial and error, obscene amounts of coffee, and a relentless determination to crash through walls and repeatedly pick herself back up, Qatarina has now produced hundreds of successful books (of her own and for clients), coached dozens of clients, built her business from zero to six figures and beyond, and been featured on numerous media outlets.

Shortly after starting Wandering Words Media, Qatarina got heavily involved with what is now known as the Tya Mindset Practice™ and went on to join Tya Mastery and also become a Tya coach, teaching others how master the practice of "Trusting Your Abundance."

When she isn't writing, reading, or coaching, she is likely lifting weights, sweating in a hot yoga class, eating sushi with her daughter, Ora Wanders—a published author at ten years of age—or jumping out of a plane in the Rocky Mountains.

To learn more about her work, please visit:

www.QatarinaWanders.com

COMING SOON...

Trainwreck Relationships And How To Avoid Them: Shift Your Mindset To Have Better Relationships & Break Free From The Vicious Cycle Once And For All

Address those red flags early on! When you sense the beginning of a train wreck, make sure you leap off for something more promising. You'll be glad you did!

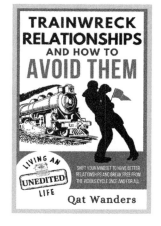

Do you ever feel like every time you start to develop a solid bond with someone, some tragic inevitably occurs?

Join the club.

In *Trainwreck Relationships And How To Avoid Them*, author and sex-coach Qatarina Wanders shares her personal stories —as well as those of her clients—of repeated romantic disasters before finally finding an approach to love that has proven true for almost two decades.

"Not all endings are happy ones" has always seemed like just another part of life—inescapable. But it doesn't have to stay that way.

Do you find yourself constantly setting expectations only to have them shattered again and again?

Fear of being duped into another marriage or commitment can leave us feeling anxious about rushing head-first into the unknown—but the world isn't perfect, so what are your best options? Have no fear! This book provides easy-to-follow guidance on navigating ahead in treacherous terrain.

Every relationship has its difficulties, but also its lessons, and sometimes we miss the point because our mindset is all wrong.

Qatarina deftly uses her wisdom from experience to direct you in how NOT to repeat mistakes on your path.

It is one thing when someone gives us advice on a topic or problem that affects them, but it is quite another when they have learned from experience. Qatarina's advice isn't just well-researched and logically sound—it also has an element of personal integrity that sets the book apart from others in its category.

Let this incredibly candid and informative book be your guiding light.

Order Now!

"Be the unicorn wh~
you set out to do!" ~Qa~

◆Crush Your Goals

◆Master Manifestation

◆Be Productive AF

Are you a busy, active, and perhaps somewhat overwhelmed, entrepreneur?

This planner was designed to help you organize your life in the areas you need it most. It helps with not only your daily to-do list, but also intention setting, visualizations, affirmations, manifestations, financial tracking, and even your exercise regimen. Set a plan for your year! And then actually achieve what you plan because you organize your entire year month by month, week by week, and day by day. By breaking everything down into bite-size pieces, your goals become more attainable.

Those who actually achieve what they set out to do tend to be as rare as a certain mythical creature...

★So be that unicorn!★

SEX-HELP BOOKS

Sex is a taboo subject in our society. We are taught to hide our sexual desires and not talk about them, which makes it hard to explore new things or even ask for what you want.

It's easy to feel like the only one who likes certain kinks, or feels guilty when you think of doing something outside the norm. But you're not alone!

Sex is not a dirty word or something that should make you feel guilty. Learn to embrace your own sexuality without feeling shame over what turns you on (or off). This book also covers:

• how to communicate with partners about sex without being awkward

• finding empowerment to help prevent victimization

• why open relationships might just be right for some people

• which orgasms you might be missing out on (and how to have them!)

We all want to have amazing sex, but we don't always know how to get there. If you're not having orgasms or having them too rarely, then you need this book in your life.

You deserve pleasure!

It's time to stop feeling guilty about what turns us on and start embracing our kinks with confidence.

I've been there too. In my early twenties, I felt like something was wrong with me because I wasn't experiencing as much pleasure as everyone else seemed to be doing. That's why I wrote this book...to give other sexually empowered women (and men) the tools needed to make sure that they're getting everything they need from their sexual experiences.

In *Sexually Empowered*, I'll show you how to accept your sexuality, understand what makes you tick sexually, learn how to have better sex with multiple partners in an open and honest way while still being ethical (and hopefully fun) about it!

Moving Beyond Slut-Shaming

Get a taste of the forbidden fruit...

Stop being afraid of what others think...

Are you tired of feeling guilty about your sexuality?

The world is changing and so are we. We're living in a time where sexual liberation is more important than ever before, but it can be hard to figure out how to do that when society tells us otherwise. This book will help you explore your kinks and find the best way for them to fit into your life without guilt or shame. You deserve better than this!

It doesn't matter if you're single or not, monogamous or polyamorous, gay or straight—whatever kind of sex life you want is possible with these tips and tricks from experts who have been there themselves.

Slut-shaming is a term used to describe the act of making someone feel guilty or ashamed for their sexual behavior. And it's not just about wearing revealing clothes, but also includes any type of expression that breaks from traditional romantic norms. In this book, I share my personal story of feeling guilty about being sexual and also cover the facts about slut-shaming and ways to get past it... and OWN IT.

Moving Beyond Slut-Shaming is a book about embracing your kinks and sexuality without feeling guilty. In this book, I'll teach you how to have multiple partners in an open and honest way, learn that sex is meant to be embraced and enjoyed (and how), and that it's nothing to be ashamed of. You'll also find out how being ethical can make for more fun!

MY JOURNEY THAT LED TO THE TYA PRACTICE

Searching for Venus: A Vagabond Lesbian Memoir

"A gripping combination of sexuality and spirituality . . . It's easy to see pieces of ourselves shining through this compelling story that centers on the struggle for inner peace." -Spiritual Biz Magazine

An Esoteric Adventure of Romance, Travel, & Subculture

The search for the Divine Feminine begins within. This is my life story told through a fictionalized character named Ruth. I wrote this WAY before the Tya Practice was created, but the principles still show up throughout.

YOGA BOOKS

Overcoming Chronic Pain Through Yoga: The Therapeutic Art of Mindful Movement

Yoga for YOU: Crafting A Yoga Practice For Your Personal Needs

RESOURCES

THE TYA PRACTICE

If you are interested in learning more about the Stream and the Tya Practice I mentioned at the beginning of the book, check out www.theStreamofDavid.com and/or email me at qatarina@qatwanders.com to schedule a call to get you involved.

A little bit about the practice:

Join us in the Tya Practice today and get on the road to living a life of fulfillment and clarity.

It's not about creating a daydream. It's time to live in your dreams. The Tya Practice is the refuge you've been seeking where living a fulfilled life is easier than you ever imagined.

Ever wonder what it would be like if you could embrace all of yourself instead of judging icky bits? Tya Practice says it's time we think differently about our thoughts, habits, emotions . . . basically anything that makes us feel uncomfortable or inadequate.

The Tya Practice is a new operating system for humanity. It stands for Trust Your Abundance and draws on the ideals of vibrational flow, self-love, and acceptance. Join this online community to learn how to transform your life with accepting self-lessons that will heal your mind, body, and soul.

Get started now!

In addition, if you are interested in my Tya-inspired coaching options, you can also email me at qatarina@ qatwanders.com for more information.

REFERENCES

- Forbes.com

- Crisis Prevention Institute

- Adfam. (2010). Setting and Keeping Boundaries. Retrieved from https://www.adfam.org.uk/cms/docs/

Adfam%20handout%20-%20setting%20and%20keep
ing%20boundaries.pdf

• Cloud, H., & Townsend, J. (2011). BOUNDARIES:
When to Say Yes, When to Say No to Take Control of
Your Life. Retrieved from http://cwjc.net/wp-content/
uploads/2013/01/Boundaries.pdf

• Edutopia. (n.d.). Healthy Boundaries, Healthy
Children. Retrieved from http://www.edutopia.org/sites/
default/files/resources/stw-glenview-healthy-
boundaries.pdf

• Katherine, A. (n.d.). How to Create Healthy
Boundaries. Retrieved from https://www.uky.edu/hr/
sites/www.uky.edu.hr/files/wellness/images/
Conf14_Boundaries.pdf

• Therapist Aid LLC. (2016). What are personal
boundaries. Retrieved from https://uhs.berkeley.edu/
sites/default/files/relationships_personal_boundaries.pd

• https://goop.com/wellness/relationships/setting-
healthy-boundaries-with-parents/

• https://www.empoweringparents.com/article/parental-
roles-how-to-set-healthy-boundaries-with-your-child/

WANDERING WORDS

M E D I A